Top 25 locator map (continues on inside back cover)

←

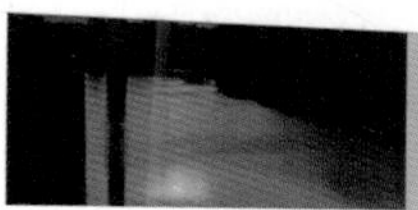

CityPack Washington

MARY CASE AND BRUCE WALKER

If you have any comments or suggestions for this guide you can contact the editor at *Citypack@theAA.com*

AA Publishing
Find out more about AA Publishing and the wide range of services the AA provides by visiting our website at www.theAA.com

About This Book

KEY TO SYMBOLS

- Map reference to the accompanying fold-out map and Top 25 locator map
- Address
- Telephone number
- Opening/closing times
- Restaurant or café on premises or nearby
- Nearest railway station
- Nearest subway (tube) station
- Nearest bus route
- Nearest riverboat or ferry stop
- Facilities for visitors with disabilities
- Admission charges: Expensive (over $9), Moderate ($3–9), and Inexpensive ($2 or less).
- Other nearby places of interest
- Other practical information
- ➤ Indicates the page where you will find a fuller description
- Tourist information

ORGANIZATION

This guide is divided into six chapters:

- Planning Ahead, Getting There
- Living Washington—Washington Now, Washington Then, Time to Shop, Out and About, Walks, Washington by Night
- Washington's Top 25 Sights
- Washington's Best—best of the rest
- Where To—detailed listings of restaurants, hotels, shops, and nightlife
- Travel Facts—practical information

In addition, easy-to-read side panels provide extra facts and snippets, highlights of places to visit and invaluable practical advice.

The colours of the tabs on the page corners match the colours of the triangles aligned with the chapter names on the contents page opposite.

MAPS

The fold-out map in the wallet at the back of this book is a comprehensive street plan of Washington. The first (or only) grid reference given for each attraction refers to this map. **The Top 25 locator map** found on the inside front and back covers of the book itself is for quick reference. It shows the Top 25 Sights, described on pages 26–50, which are clearly plotted by number (1–25, not page number) across the city. The second map reference given for the Top 25 Sights refers to this map.

Contents

PLANNING AHEAD, GETTING THERE 4 – 7

LIVING WASHINGTON 8 – 24

WASHINGTON'S TOP 25 SIGHTS 25 – 50

1 Arlington National Cemetery *26*
2 John F. Kennedy Center *27*
3 Lincoln Memorial *28*
4 Phillips Collection *29*
5 Vietnam Veterans Memorial *30*
6 National Geographic Society *31*
7 The White House *32*
8 Washington Monument *33*
9 F. D. R. & Jefferson Memorials *34*
10 US Holocaust Memorial Museum *35*
11 National Museum of American History *36*
12 Bureau of Engraving & Printing *37*
13 Freer & Arthur M. Sackler Galleries *38*
14 Smithsonian Institution *39*
15 FBI Building *40*
16 National Archives *41*
17 National Gallery of Art *42*
18 National Air & Space Museum *43*
19 US Botanic Gardens *44*
20 US Capitol *45*
21 Union Station *46*
22 US Supreme Court Building *47*
23 Library of Congress *48*
24 National Shrine of the Immaculate Conception *49*
25 Cedar Hill *50*

WASHINGTON'S BEST 51 – 62

WHERE TO 63 – 88

TRAVEL FACTS 89 – 93

INDEX 94 – 95

CREDITS AND ACKNOWLEDGMENTS 96

Planning Ahead

When to go

There is no bad time to visit Washington. Spring is busiest, when the city's cherry trees are in blossom. October and November bring brilliant foliage. Summer, although crowded and sweltering, sees a chock-a-block calendar of special events.

TIME

Washington is on Eastern Standard Time. Clocks go forward one hour in April and go back in late-October.

AVERAGE DAILY MAXIMUM TEMPERATURES

JAN	FEB	MAR	APR	MAY	JUN	JUL	AUG	SEP	OCT	NOV	DEC
42°F	44°F	53°F	64°F	75°F	83°F	87°F	84°F	78°F	67°F	55°F	45°F
6°C	7°C	12°C	18°C	24°C	28°C	31°C	29°C	26°C	19°C	13°C	7°C

Spring (mid-March to May) is extremely pleasant, with flowers and trees in bloom throughout the city.
Summer (June to early September) is hot and humid, with temperatures sometimes reaching 95°F or more.
Autumn (mid-September to November) is comfortable, and sometimes bracing.
Winter (December to mid-March) varies from year to year: It can be extremely cold or surprisingly warm. The occasional snowfall shuts the city down.

WHAT'S ON

January *Antiques Show* (☎ 202/234-0700).
Martin Luther King, Jr. Birthday Observation (☎ 202/727-1186).
February *President's Day* (☎ 202/619-7275).
Chinese New Year's Parade (☎ 202/638-1041).
March *St. Patrick's Day Festival* (☎ 202/637-2484).
Organist's Bach Marathon (☎ 202/363-2202).
Smithsonian Kite Flying Festival (☎ 202/357-2700).
April *National Cherry Blossom Festival* (☎ 202/661-7599).
White House Spring Garden Tour (☎ 202/456-7041).
May *Washington National Cathedral Flower Mart* (☎ 202/537-6200).
Mother's Day: Capitol Hill Restoration Society House Tour (☎ 202/543-0425).
Marine Band Summer Concert Series (☎ 202/433-4011).
July *Smithsonian Festival of American Folklife* (☎ 202/357-2700).
Independence Day (4 Jul ☎ 202/619-7222).
September *National Symphony Orchestra Labor Day Concert* (☎ 202/467-4600).
Adams-Morgan Day (☎ 202/321-0938).
Black Family Reunion (☎ 202/737-0120).
October *Washington International Horse Show* (☎ 301/840-0281).
Marine Corps Marathon (☎ 800/786-8762).
Taste of DC Festival (☎ 202/724-5430).
November *Veterans' Day* (☎ 202/745-8000).
December *People's Christmas Tree Lighting* (☎ 202/224-3069).

Washington Online

www.dcnrhs.org/union
This is the site for Union Station, Washington's major rail link, with schedules, visitor information, directions, and transportation services.

www.si.edu
The Smithsonian Institution site features a directory of its 16 museums, schedules of events and exhibits, information about research and publications, and a link to the gift shop.

www.supershuttle.com
This site belongs to an airport shuttle service. You can make reservations for travel to any of the three airports.

www.supremecourtus.gov
The Supreme Court site has information about cases on the docket, exhibitions, and how to watch the court in session.

www.washington.org
This site is presented by the Washington, DC, Convention and Tourism board. You can make hotel reservations, gather information about the different neighbourhoods, and find out about annual events.

www.washingtonpost.com
The newspaper's site features a visitor's guide, including airport status reports, calendar of events, and reviews of entertainment venues and restaurants.

www.dcpages.com
This comprehensive site features virtual tours of top tourist sites as well as giving information about area restaurants, shops, festivals and events, and DC weather.

www.senate.gov
www.house.gov
These are the sites for each body of Congress; information on upcoming votes, leadership, history, and how to visit.

GOOD TRAVEL SITES

www.fodors.com
A complete travel-planning site. You can research prices and weather; book air tickets, cars and rooms; ask questions (and get answers) from fellow travellers; and find links to other sites.

www.wmata.com
The Washington Metropolitan Transit Authority site features a map of the Metro system, plus information on delays and holiday schedules.

CYBERCAFÉS

Kramerbooks & Afterwoods Café & Grille
F4 · 1517 Connecticut Avenue NW, Dupont Circle · 202/387-1400 · Mon–Fri 7.30AM–1AM, Sat–Sun 24 hours · 15 minutes of free email at the bar

Cyberstop Café
F3 · 1513 17th Street, NW · 202/234-2470 · 7AM–midnight · $5.99 per half hour, $7.99 per hour

Interactive Cybercafe US
E3 · 1217 22nd Street NW · 202/861-5858 · Daily 4PM–2AM

Getting There

METRO TRANSFERS

To transfer to a bus after leaving the Metro, get a transfer from the dispenser next to the escalator that goes down to the train level.

MONEY

The unit of currency is the dollar (= 100 cents). Notes (bills) comes in denominations of $1, $5, $10, $20, $50, and $100; coins are 25¢ (a quarter), 10¢ (a dime), 5¢ (a nickel) and 1¢ (a penny).
Sales tax in Washington, DC, is 5.75 percent, hotel tax 14.5 percent (9.75 percent in Virginia) and restaurant tax 10 percent in addition to the bill.

$5

$10

$50

$100

ARRIVING

Flying time to Washington, District of Columbia, is 1 hour from New York, 5 hours 40 minutes from Los Angeles, and 8 hours from London. The major airports include Ronald Reagan National Airport, Dulles International Airport, and Baltimore-Washington International Airport.

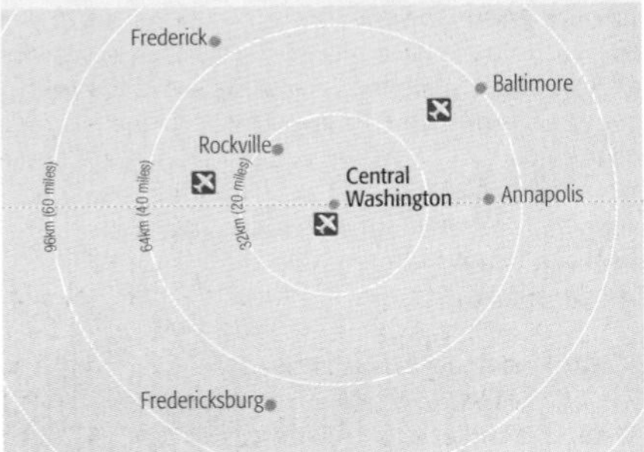

From Ronald Reagan National Airport

Ronald Reagan National Airport (☎ 703/417-8000) is in Virginia, 6.4km (4mi) south of downtown. A taxi to downtown takes around 20 minutes and costs around $16.25. SuperShuttle (☎ 800/809-7080) offers an airport-to-door service for $22 per person 24 hours a day. The blue and yellow Metro lines run from the airport to downtown, with stations next to terminals B and C (🕔 Mon–Thu 5.30AM–midnight; Fri, Sat 8AM–1AM; Sun 8AM–midnight). Fare cards ($1.10 to $45, available in day passes and other periods) can be bought from machines on level 2 near the pedestrian bridges linking the two terminals. Metro information ☎ 202/637- 7000. Private Car (☎ 800/685-0888) will arrange for a car or limousine to meet you at the airport. Cost is around $45 for a sedan and $55 for a limousine, plus a 15 percent gratuity.

From Dulles International Airport

Dulles International Airport (☎ 703/572-2700) is 42km (26mi) west of Washington. A taxi to the city takes around 40 minutes and costs around $45. The Washington Flyer (☎ 703/685-

1400) goes from the airport to the Convention Center at New York Avenue and 11th Street NW. Buses leave the airport every half hour around the clock. The 45-minute trip costs $16 ($26 round-trip). An inter-airport service is available between Dulles and Reagan National airports for the same price. Cash, Visa, and MasterCard are accepted. SuperShuttle (☎ 800/809-7080) offers a 24-hour door-to-door service for $22 per person plus $10 for each additional person. Private Car (☎ 800/685-0888) will arrange for a car or limousine to meet you at the airport; cost is around $73 for a sedan and $81 for a limousine, plus a 15 percent gratuity.

From BWI Airport

Baltimore-Washington International Airport (☎ 410/859-7100) is in Maryland, 40km (25mi) northeast of Washington. A taxi from the airport takes around 45 minutes and costs $55–$60. SuperShuttle (☎ 800/809-7080) offers a 24-hour airport-to-door service that costs $28 plus $5 for each additional person. Free shuttle buses run between airline terminals and the train station. Amtrak (☎ 800/872-7245) and MARC (☎ 800/325-7245) trains run between the airport and Union Station, Mon–Fri 6AM–midnight. The 40-minute ride costs $17 on Amtrak and $5 on MARC. Private Car (☎ 800/685-0888) has two counters at the airport; you'll pay $63 for a sedan or $68 for a limousine, plus a 15 percent gratuity.

Getting Around

The city's subway system, the Metro, is one of the cleanest and safest in the country. You need a farecard to ride, both to enter and exit. Farecard machines, located in the stations, take coins and $1, $5, $10, and $20 notes. The bus system covers a much wider area than the Metro. The fare within the city is $1.10. Taxi fares are based on a zone system. The base fare for one passenger within a zone is $4, with a $1.50 charge for each extra passenger and a $1 surcharge Mon–Fri 4–6.40PM. Zone maps are displayed in all cabs.

For more information on getting around ➤ 91.

INSURANCE

Check your policy and buy any necessary supplements. It is vital that travel insurance covers medical expenses, in addition to accident, trip cancellation, baggage loss, and theft. Check the policy covers any continuing treatment for a chronic condition.

DRIVING IN DC

Driving in Washington is for the patient only; gridlock is often worsened by construction.
The speed limit in the city is 25mph (40km/h), unless otherwise stated. Seat belts are mandatory for the driver and front-seat passenger. Before you park on city streets, check for signs to make sure it is permitted.

VISITORS WITH DISABILITIES

Museums and other public buildings are usually accessible to wheelchair users, with many ramps and elevators. Wheelchair access to Metro trains is via elevators from the street; details at www.wmata.com.
Information on various DC locations can be found at www.disabilityguide.com.

AND SLAVE IS DESPOTISM. NOTHING
IS MORE CERTAINLY WRITTEN IN THE
BOOK OF FATE THAN THAT THESE
PEOPLE ARE TO BE FREE.
A GENERAL PLAN.

Living Washington

Washington Now *10–15*

Washington Then *16–17*

Time to Shop *18–19*

Out and About *20–21*

Walks *22–23*

Washington by Night *24*

Washington Now

A time for fun at the White House: the traditional Easter Egg Roll along Pennsylvania Avenue

It cannot be said that life has gone on as usual since the 9/11 terrorist attacks on the US. The city is still feeling the emotional and economic impact of the event. But the crash of one of the three hijacked planes into the Pentagon, just across the river in Virginia, is only one among many awesome events that have unfolded here; the presence of numerous memorials and monuments tells you that what happens in Washington becomes a part of the nation's history.

You may well find that a dip in the numbers of tourists has been a boon. At this writing, bargains abound and queues are somewhat shorter at

NEIGHBOURHOODS

• Washington's neighbourhoods are as diverse as those in Paris and London. From the brick sidewalks, antique stores, and high-end properties of Georgetown, to the chic 19th-century town houses of Capitol Hill, to ethnic Adams Morgan with its street musicians and Ethiopian restaurants, the city presents many different sides. Residential areas such as Woodley Park and Cleveland Park offer wonderful examples of Victorian houses and bungalows. Quiet blocks of appealing brownstones lie adjacent to Dupont Circle, a busy urban restaurant district. Foggy Bottom, near the State Department and the Kennedy Center, surprises with its understated charm.

GRACIOUS CITY

• The influence of Washington's original urban designer, Pierre Charles L'Enfant, has been enormous, and his vision of a gracious city with airy vistas and wide thoroughfares linking impressive buildings and monuments is the city you find today. Oddly, given his legacy, he lasted only a year in the post. Appointed by George Washington in 1791, he was sacked 12 months later.

The National Statuary Hall in the US Capitol: A famous citizen is represented from each state

popular destinations. You may get closer to the Hope Diamond than you ever dreamed.

Certain parts of the city—including the areas around the White House, the Supreme Court and the buildings on Capitol Hill—have always had heightened security, with visitors asked to provide photo identification before entering most buildings. Now there are more metal detectors than ever before. Nonetheless, in keeping with democratic tradition, government buildings are still open to the public, and government business is conducted in plain sight.

In keeping with the spirit of resilience, Washington's mood is enthusiastic, and the city continues to welcome visitors and move with an optimistic beat, one in which the current administration always feels fresh and new, and young people are everywhere—newly minted interns, lobbyists, politicians, and lawyers. The essential qualities of Washington never change—it's a living city with a sense of history.

What's new? Political junkies may be most interested in the current residents at the White House

Above: *the US Capitol and Grant Statue beyond the Reflecting Pool*
Above centre: *inside the Capitol—the Great Rotunda*

or elected officials in Congress, who make headlines at work and play. The city is never without political intrigue or spectacle, as the near daily appearance of official motorcades to and from the White House attests. International relations are always on the front burner, with diplomats and world leaders coming and going along Embassy Row. Sports fans can keep an eye out for basketball megastar Michael Jordan, owner of the Wizards and a high-profile city resident.

For everyone else, the most appealing DC residents dwell far from Capitol Hill. In 2000 Washington became the home of two pandas from China. Mei Xiang and Tian Tian, bought in as replacements for the beloved Ling-Ling and Hsing Hsing, have stolen the hearts of Washingtonians and visitors alike. Baby giraffes, elephants, hippos, and gorillas, to name a few, show up from time to time, so there's frequently a fresh face, snout, or trunk to watch.

As always, a visit to Washington affords a chance to take in world-class arts events, from performances by the National Symphony Orchestra to the dance and opera productions that fill up the

A TALE OF TWO CITIES

- President John F. Kennedy uttered the most telling quote about the city's hybrid personality when he remarked that Washington had a combination of "Northern hospitality and Southern efficiency."

Kennedy Center. Washington is a thriving theatre town, with shows originating in Broadway and London coming to visit and the occasional Broadway-bound show trying out here. The critically acclaimed regional theatres at the world-renowned Arena Stage and Woolly Mammoth Theater Company offer fine productions of the work of cutting-edge playwrights.

Above: *awesome architecure—the Main Reading Room in the Library of Congress*

PLEASANTVILLE

• Washington is small enough to walk across in a day. Downtown avenues bustle with businessmen and lawyers. The National Mall offers a lushly planted vista for jogging and walking, where you can get up close to the stately monuments. Unlike most cities its size, Washington lacks concrete canyons; strict building regulations forbid skyscrapers that would block out the sun. This means the downtown area in particular, while busy and urgent, retains a human scale. Washington is also a city of gardens, the legacy of Lady Bird Johnson, who splashed flowers in unlikely places, and of the Japanese government, who gave the city the first of its famous cherry trees. Smaller neighbourhoods and side streets add to the overall charm.

MADELEINE K. ALBRIGHT

• Though she's no longer secretary of state, Madeleine K. Albright maintains a high profile in Washington. She holds an endowed chair at Georgetown University, where she is the Mortara Distinguished Professor of Diplomacy. As she was when in office, she's an outspoken proponent of human rights and an accomplished hostess of A-list dinner parties.

Above: *boutiques, restaurants, trains, and more in Union Station*

Likewise, the permanent collections of the National Gallery, Hirshhorn, and other Smithsonian museums are filled with choice objects, paintings, and sculptures, as are the private museums such as the Phillips Collection and Corcoran Gallery. Major authors stop here on book tours (seemingly there is no end of politicians with new books). Thinkers and scientists alike give public lectures about contemporary issues.

While it would seem impossible to make old monuments new again, several choice Washington sites are being renovated and reopened, including the National Archives building, home of the Constitution and the Declaration of Independence, and the Botanical Gardens. Not to be outdone, the most widely

LANDSCAPER'S LEGACY

• Thanks to acclaimed 19th-century landscape architect Frederick Law Olmsted, Washington is full of green spaces and public parks. The 40km (25mi) long Rock Creek Park was established in 1890 for the "benefit and enjoyment of the people of the United States" and served as an inspiration for future national parks.

recognized symbol of the city, the Washington Monument, has emerged from its recent makeover, and the view from the top has never been better.

Although it's built on a grid (letter streets go east–west, number streets go north–south, avenues are diagonal) there's nothing truly regular about Washington's street scene. An international city, drawing diplomats, students, and business people from around the globe, Washington is the backdrop for large city-wide political actions and demonstrations, as well as smaller protests by special interest groups. You never know when you might come upon followers of Falun Gong or the Free Tibet movement, to name just a few, handing out literature for their cause. In the case of larger demonstrations, Washington plays its part as witness to civil rights rallies, philosophical calls to arms, and emerging political concerns.

To walk down the streets or on the Mall in this city is to be reminded that Washington is a place where people come to be seen and heard by the rest of the world.

Above: *John F. Kennedy Center, the Hall of States*
Above left: *an elegant address in Georgetown*

VITAL STATISTICS

- Washington has more than 60 radio and television stations.
- The Washington Monument is the world's tallest masonry structure, at 169m (555ft).
- The National Building Museum has the world's tallest Corinthian columns, at 23m (75ft).
- Washington's largest employer is the federal government, with 240,000 employees.

Washington Then

Left to centre: *L'Enfant's plan of Washington in 1791; President John Adams; the capture of Washington, 1814*

1812 US declares war on Britain in response to the impressment of sailors from American ships and border disputes in Canada.

1814 The British sack Washington, burning the White House and the Capitol. The War of 1812 ends with Treaty of Ghent, ratified in late 1814.

1846 Congress accepts James Smithson's bequest and establishes the Smithsonian Institution.

1850 The slave trade is abolished in the District of Columbia.

1863 President Abraham Lincoln's Emancipation Proclamation frees the nation's slaves. Many former slaves move to Washington.

1865 Lincoln is assassinated during a performance at Ford's Theater.

1867 Howard University is chartered by Congress to educate blacks.

1876 The nation's centennial is celebrated with a fair in Philadelphia. Fifty-six train cars are filled with material to be donated to the Smithsonian.

1901 The McMillan Commission oversees the city's beautification.

EARLY DAYS

In 1770 President George Washington was authorized by Congress to build a Federal City. The following year he hired Pierre Charles L'Enfant to design a city beside the Potomac River. According to legend, he sited the US Capitol in the exact centre of the 13 original states. By 1800 President Adams was able to occupy the unfinished White House, and Congress met in the Capitol, also unfinished. The population was by then around 3,000.

DOWN THE WIRE

In 1844 Samuel F. B. Morse transmitted the first telegraph message from the Capitol to Baltimore, Maryland.

1908 Trains run to the new Union Station.

1958 The East Front extension of the Capitol begins, adding 102 offices.

1961 President John F. Kennedy plans the renovation of Pennsylvania Avenue. Residents are given the right to vote in presidential elections.

1968–73 Demonstrations against the Vietnam War are held on the National Mall.

1974 The Watergate Hotel becomes infamous as the site of the bungled Republican robbery attempt on Democratic headquarters. President Richard Nixon resigns as a result of the ensuing cover-up.

1976 The Metrorail opens.

1981 President Ronald Reagan is shot and injured outside the Washington Hilton.

1990 Mayor Sharon Pratt Dixon Kelly becomes the first black woman to lead a major US city.

2001 Terrorists highjack a passenger plane from Dulles Airport on September 11 and crash it into the Pentagon, killing 64 people in the jet and 190 on the ground.

Above left: *Martin Luther King, Jr.—"I Have a Dream"*
Above: *President Ronald Reagan is shot*

"I HAVE A DREAM"

On 28 August 1963 Martin Luther King, Jr., delivered his vision of racial harmony from the steps of the Lincoln Memorial to a crowd of 200,000. Born in 1929, King had entered the ministry in 1955. As pastor of the Dexter Avenue Baptist Church in Montgomery, Alabama, he became the figurehead of the organized non-violent civil-rights protests to end discrimination laws. His "I Have a Dream" speech ended a march on Washington by blacks and whites calling for reform. King was awarded the Nobel Peace Prize in 1964. His last sermon was at Washington National Cathedral in 1968–he was shot five days later in Memphis.

Time to Shop

Below and centre: *the Georgetown Park mall; Borders book store at 1801 L Street NW*

Well-heeled Washingtonians outfit themselves and their homes at the high-end Nieman-Marcus and Saks Fifth Avenue and at mainstream stores like Target—you'll find it all in DC. Boutiques and

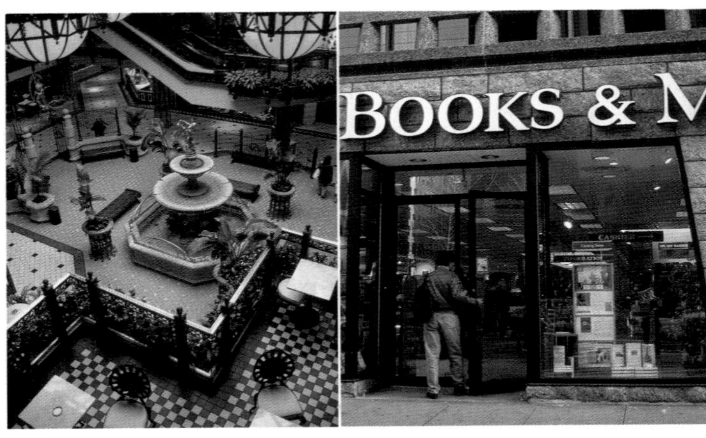

niche shops sell T-shirts and toe rings or the conservative tweeds and button-down Oxford-cloth shirts to college students and their grandparents. Georgetown shops are stuffed with three centuries of antique household items, furniture, and artwork. Across town, along the U Street Corridor is the city's best selection of contemporary furniture, as well as vintage clothes. An unusually high number of rug dealers can sell you throw rugs, runners, or another unique oriental.

The city is also rich in bookshops, featuring many outlets of the major chains such as Borders and Barnes & Noble and the DC-wide Olssons, as well as bookshops that cater specially to travellers, mystery readers, gays and lesbians, and history buffs, to name a few. Major authors visit Washington regularly on book tours. In addition to selling books, the city's independent bookstores such as Kramer Books and Politics & Prose frequently provide comfortable cafes and browsing sites for booklovers and their friends.

PATTERNS FROM AFRICA

You may be intrigued by the vibrant hues and patterns of the kente cloth clothing worn by chic African-Americans in DC. Hand-woven in Ghana, it's available in bolts to sew with or made up into outfits from several good sources. Start your search at the National Museum of African Art (☎ 202/357-4600).

What really distinguishes shopping in DC, however, is the abundance of art works, reproductions, and trinkets for sale at the many museum shops across town. You can pick up

Below and left: *window shopping in Georgetown*

Native American pieces at the Department of Interior, or a history of the Holocaust at the Holocaust Museum's gift shop. The Smithsonian museums offer everything from CDs of American jazz to reproduction period jewellery to 18th-century toys. The Hirshhorn sells art supplies, postcards, and posters, and books about art. The Air and Space Museum offers glow-in-the-dark stars and planet stickers, and the kind of freeze-dried food eaten by orbiting astronauts. The National Gallery has a huge selection of reproductions in the form of posters, books, catalogues, post cards, and slides. African-American art, including masks and sculpture, is available in museums and galleries. Art collectors should visit the Dupont Circle galleries.

Not least, Washington is a good place to buy food products and household items culled from the surrounding regions: Virginia peanuts, ham from Carolina and Kentucky, Pennsylvania quilts, and Appalachian handcrafts such as hand-made brooms and corn-husk dolls.

POLITICAL EPHEMERA

Election year or not, DC is a ready source of campaign ephemera–buttons, bumper stickers, matchbooks with party logos, and the like. At bookshops, museum gift shops, and street vendors alike, reproductions and original memorabilia abound. Looking for pewter flatware and candlesticks used by 18th-century administrations? A tacky T-shirt commenting on the latest Washington scandal? Who can resist the salt and pepper shakers shaped like the Washington Monument or campaign buttons designed for FDR? For this kind of Americana, there's no place like DC.

Out and About

PERSONAL GUIDES

A Tour de Force
✉ Box 2782,
Washington, DC 20013
☎ 703/525-2948

Guide Service of Washington
✉ 733 15th Street, Suite 1040, Washington, DC 20005 ☎ 202/628-2842

Anthony S. Pitch
The knowledgeable and entertaining Anthony Pitch leads walks through historic Georgetown, Victorian Adams-Morgan, Lafayette Square, and from Capitol Hill to the White House.
☎ 301/294-9514;
www.dcsightseeing.com

Sonny Odom
The person to call if photography is your thing.
☎ 703/379-1633;
sonnyodom@comcast.net

INFORMATION

FREDERICKSBURG
Distance 80km (50mi)
Journey Time 1–2 hours
Amtrak from Union Station
By Car South on I-95 to exit 130A and follow signs to the visitors centre.
706 Caroline Street
☎ 540/373-1776;
www.fredericksburgvirginia.net Daily 9–5

ORGANIZED SIGHTSEEING

Washington has plenty of guided walking and bus tours. Gray Line buses take in the major sites and also travel to Mount Vernon and Alexandria (☎ 301/386-8300). The Discovery Store Walk takes you through Chinatown and Washington's

original residential and commercial areas (☎ 202/639-0908). Smithsonian walking and bus tours through neighbourhoods are often topical (☎ 202/357-2700). Hop-on hop-off tourmobiles have stops at most sites in this guide (☎ 202/554-7950). Old Town Trolleys run every half-hour, and you can board them at any of their stops (☎ 301/985-3021). The National Park Service produces a brochure on the Black History National Recreation Trail (☎ 202/619-7222).

EXCURSIONS

FREDERICKSBURG

The 40-block National Historic District in this charming Virginia town comprises the house George Washington bought for his mother, a 1752 plantation, James Monroe's law offices, an early apothecary shop, and the Georgian Chatham Manor, overlooking the Rappahannock River. Many Civil War battles were waged in and around town, and you can walk in the battlefields and in nearby wilderness parks. Antiques and rare-books shops and art galleries line the streets. Start at the well-marked visitors centre, which dispenses maps and advice.

Mount Vernon

George Washington's ancestral Virginia estate is the nation's second-most visited historic house after the White House. The Ladies Association, formed in 1853 to preserve the estate, is credited with starting the historic preservation movement in the US. The mansion overlooks the Potomac River and is built of yellow pine painted to resemble stone. The ornate interior is furnished with fine arts and memorabilia from the last years of Washington's life. The outbuildings re-create the spaces of a self-sufficient 18th-century farm, including the smokehouse and laundry, outside kitchen, and slave quarters. On the river side, don't miss the view of George and Martha Washington's tomb.

Left: *Mount Vernon, home of George Washington*
Below: *colonial Alexandria*

Old Town, Alexandria

With its well-preserved colonial seaport architecture, this Virginia community is a sophisticated version of small-town America. Old Town is easily covered on foot and includes hundreds of colonial buildings, many open to the public. The Torpedo Factory Arts Center houses Historic Alexandria, which conducts local archaeological research, and artisans are often on hand to discuss the exhibits, as well as their own work. Start at Ramsay House Visitors Center (☒ 221 King Street ☎ 703/838-4200), where you can get tickets to historic properties, parking permits, and walking tour brochures.

INFORMATION

Mount Vernon
Distance 27.4km (17mi)
Journey Time 40 minutes
☎ 703/780-2000; www.mountvernon.org
Mar, Sep–Oct: daily 9–5. Apr–Aug: 8–5. Nov–Feb: 9–4
Tourmobile, Gray Line
By car Take the 14th Street Bridge (towards National Airport), then south on George Washington Memorial Parkway.
Potomac Spirit from Pier 4, 6th and Water Streets SW
Moderate

INFORMATION

Old Town, Alexandria
Distance 9.7km (6mi)
Journey Time 20 minutes
King Street Station, then DASH bus AT2 or AT5 eastbound
By car Take the 14th Street Bridge (towards National Airport), then south on George Washington Parkway to King Street.
By bike Start at Lincoln Memorial and cross Memorial Bridge heading south to Alexandria.

Walks

PRESIDENTIAL ROUTE

After the Inauguration, the president and his entourage descend the west face of the Capitol and proceed, in cars or on foot, up Pennsylvania Avenue to the White House. This walk takes the same route.

INFORMATION

Distance 2.4km (1.5mi)
Time 2 hours 45 minutes
Start point ★ US Capitol
J5
Union Station
End point White House
F4
McPherson Square

THE CAPITOL TO THE WHITE HOUSE

Begin on the west steps of the Capitol building. The view takes in Washington's famous museums and monuments, from the Botanic Gardens and federal office buildings (left along Maryland Avenue), to the Washington Monument and Lincoln Memorial (directly ahead), to the domes of the National Museum of Natural History and National Gallery of Art, and the Federal Triangle complex (right).

Follow Pennsylvania Avenue, past the National Gallery of Art, the Canadian Embassy, the National Archives, and the Navy Memorial. Turn right onto the art corridor of 7th Street up to Chinatown Metro and the Friendship Arch of Washington's Asian community. Go west along G Street and turn left onto 10th Street past Ford's Theater, where Abraham Lincoln was fatally wounded in 1865. The FBI building is on the left. Turn right onto Pennsylvania Avenue. The clock tower of the Old Post Office offers an unsurpassed view. Farther up Pennsylvania is Freedom Plaza, with its stone map of L'Enfant's city plan, and Pershing Park. Turn right onto 15th Street, past the 1836 Treasury Building, which appears on the $10 note, and take a left onto Pennsylvania Avenue in front of the White House.

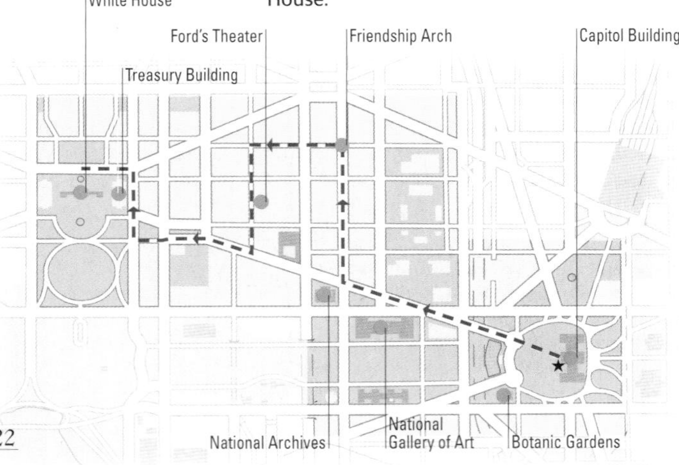

Cosmopolitan Washington

Begin at Dupont Circle Metro's Q Street exit. Go east on Q to 1700, past Thomas F. Schneider's town houses (1889–92). The Cairo Apartments (1894) at 1615 Q prompted Congress to introduce height restrictions. Turn south onto 17th Street and right onto Church Street. The altar and back wall of an early Episcopal church, destroyed by arson in 1970, frame an inviting pocket park. Turn left onto 18th and right onto P to the Italianate Patterson House (1901–3). Hartman-Cox's 1970 Euram Building, now called 21 Dupont Circle, proves that creativity can coexist with the city's strict building codes. Turn left onto New Hampshire Avenue and walk to 1307, the Historical Society of Washington. Turn right onto 20th, then left onto Massachusetts. On the left is the Walsh Mansion, purchased in 1951 by Indonesia for a tenth of the $3 million it cost to build in 1903. At 1600 21st Street is the Phillips Collection. Go on to 2118 Massachusetts Avenue and pass the courtyard of Anderson House.

After Sheridan Circle, turn right onto S Street, and stop at the Textile Museum. Walk down the Decatur Terrace Steps. Turn left onto Decatur Place, left onto Florida Avenue and continue to Connecticut Avenue and Dupont Circle Metro.

CHIC WASHINGTON

Dupont Circle is the heart of chic, single Washington and a focus of gay culture. Clubs, restaurants, bookstores, coffee shops, and boutiques line Connecticut Avenue and P Street on both sides of the Circle. Distinctive small museums and art galleries, embassies and important architecture are also on the route.

INFORMATION

Distance 4km (2.5mi)
Time 1 hour 30 minutes
Start/end point
★ Dupont Circle
F3
Dupont Circle

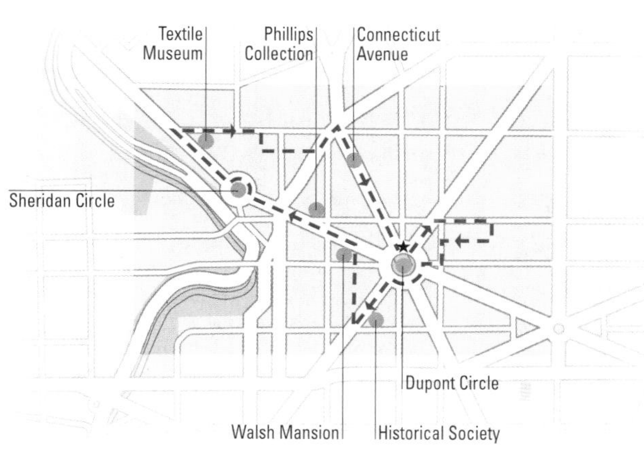

Washington by Night

Left to right: *Georgetown's nocturnal atmosphere; the Washington Monument floodlit; dusk settles on the Jefferson Memorial*

From the Driver's Seat

A car is one of the best places to experience Washington by night, when the city seems to lay out its jewelled buildings and vistas for admiration. Whether you take a cab over the bridges to glimpse the boldly illuminated silhouettes of the Jefferson and Lincoln memorials, or drive through Capitol Hill or the Mall, with the moon lighting up the Washington Monument and the Reflecting Pool, you'll experience a landscape transformed by darkness, at once inviting and prophetic. This is a city in which presidents walked at midnight, martyrs died, poets dreamed, plots were hashed, and wars contemplated. You won't forget the mood or the view.

Dinner Out

Washington can hold its own against any other major city when it comes to restaurants, and dining out while people-watching is truly fulfilling. Georgetown, although no longer DC's premiere chic watering place, still offers its share of restaurants to please every palate, as well as antiques shops, clothing boutiques, and bookshops, some of which are open past 9PM.

Hunger tamed, you can spend a pleasant half hour or so wandering the charming cobbled streets and enjoying the fountains and outdoor sculpture. Alternatively, the Exorcist Steps—made famous by the 1973 movie about demonic possession starring Ellen Burstyn and Max Von Sydow—are on M Street at Prospect Street, a short walk from the main drag.

TASTE OF BOHEMIA

The popular Adams-Morgan District is home to numerous ethnic restaurants, including many serving Washington's famed Ethiopian fare, as well as shops and bars that are open late. The bohemian mood lasts until early morning. College students, crowded out of Georgetown pubs, hang out here in packs. For a more cutting-edge evening, visit the U Street corridor, a former red-light district that is now home to jazz clubs and chic restaurants.

WASHINGTON's top 25 sights

The sights are shown on the maps on the inside front cover and inside back cover, numbered 1–25 across the city

1 Arlington National Cemetery *26*

2 John F. Kennedy Center *27*

3 Lincoln Memorial *28*

4 Phillips Collection *29*

5 Vietnam Veterans Memorial *30*

6 National Geographic Society *31*

7 The White House *32*

8 Washington Monument *33*

9 F. D. R. & Jefferson Memorials *34*

10 US Holocaust Memorial Museum *35*

11 National Museum of American History *36*

12 Bureau of Engraving & Printing *37*

13 Freer & Arthur M. Sackler Galleries *38*

14 Smithsonian Institution *39*

15 FBI Building *40*

16 National Archives *41*

17 National Gallery of Art *42*

18 National Air & Space Museum *43*

19 US Botanic Gardens *44*

20 US Capitol *45*

21 Union Station *46*

22 US Supreme Court Building *47*

23 Library of Congress *48*

24 Shrine of the Immaculate Conception *49*

25 Cedar Hill *50*

Top **25**

1

Arlington National Cemetery

HIGHLIGHTS

- Kennedy graves
- Tomb of the Unknowns
- Custis-Lee Mansion
- L'Enfant's grave
- USS Marine Memorial
- Shuttle *Challenger*
- Astronauts Memorial
- Changing of the Guard at the Tomb of the Unknowns

INFORMATION

- C6–D7, locator map A3
- ANC, Arlington, VA 22211
- 703/607-8052, www.arlingtoncemetery.org/
- Apr–Sep: daily 8–7. Oct–Mar: daily 8–5
- Free
- Excellent. Visitors with disabilities may board Tourmobile Shuttles or obtain driving permit at the Visitors Center
- Arlington Cemetery
- Tourmobile
- Lincoln Memorial (► 28), Vietnam Veterans Memorial (► 30), Francis Scott Key Bridge (► 62)
- Narrated Tourmobile Shuttle, every 20 minutes. Changing of the Guard: Apr–Sep daily on the half hour; Oct–Mar daily on the hour. Parking available at the cemetery

The national cemetery since 1883, Arlington famously contains the most visited grave in the country, that of John F. Kennedy. Rows of headstones commemorate with dignity the war dead and national heroes.

Lest we forget The first burial at the Tomb of the Unknowns occurred on 11 November 1921. This World War I soldier was joined in 1958 by honored dead from World War II and Korea and, for 15 years beginning in 1984, by a Vietnam veteran. In 1999 DNA techniques facilitated the identification of the Vietnam veteran, who was subsequently moved by his family. Sentries perform with great precision a regular Changing of the Guard ceremony.

White markers and a flame Under an eternal flame, John F. Kennedy lies next to his wife, Jacqueline Bouvier Kennedy Onassis, and two of his children who died in infancy. Nearby lies his brother, Robert Kennedy, slain in 1968, whose grave is marked by a simple white cross and a fountain. Above the Kennedy graves stands the Greek-revival Custis-Lee Mansion (also known as Arlington House), built between 1802 and 1817 by George Washington Parke Custis, grandson of Martha and step-grandson of George Washington. Just off the west corner of the house lies the grave of Pierre L'Enfant, now overlooking for eternity the Federal City that he designed in the face of difficulties that left him penniless and embittered. Throughout the 612-acre cemetery, row upon row of simple white markers recall the soldiers who gave their lives. Memorials commemorate a particular event or group of people. A 1997 memorial is dedicated to women who lost their lives in military service.

John F. Kennedy Center

With five theatres of differing sizes, this national cultural centre covers 3.2ha (8 acres) and is the jewel of the city's arts venues. The roof terrace provides a stunning 360-degree view of Washington and the Potomac.

The seat of the arts Opened in 1971, Edward Durrell Stone's simple white marble box overlooks the Potomac River next to the Watergate complex, infamous for the 1972 bungled attempt to bug the Democratic National Committee, which eventually led to President Richard Nixon's resignation. When the Kennedy Center opened, the Washington performing arts scene took a great leap forward; the opera house and concert hall especially have splendid acoustics.

Hall of States The building is sheathed in 3,759 tonnes (3,700 tons) of white Carrara marble, a gift from Italy. The Grand Foyer, 192m (630ft) long, blazes from the light of 18 Orrefors crystal chandeliers, donated by Sweden and reflected in 18.3m (60ft) high mirrors, a gift from Belgium. Overlooking theatergoers is a bust of John F. Kennedy by Robert Berks, who also designed the Albert Einstein Memorial. The expansive lobby, called the Hall of States, displays state flags arranged in the order in which the states were admitted to the Union. One end of the hall is devoted to the Millennium Stage where performances are given in the evening. The building also accommodates two stage theatres, a movie theatre, a theatre lab, and the Performing Arts Library of the Library of Congress. Many of these can be seen on a tour of the building or at intermission during a performance.

HIGHLIGHTS

- Hall of States
- View from the roof terrace
- Henri Matisse tapestries, a gift from France

INFORMATION

- E4–E5, locator map B2
- 2700 F Street NW
- 202/467-4600, 800/444-1324, www.kennedy-center.org/
- Daily for tours and performances as scheduled
- Free tours; performance ticket prices vary
- Excellent
- Encore Café, Roof Terrace Restaurant; call 202/416-8555 for hours
- Foggy Bottom. Free bus shuttle every 15 minutes 5–11.45PM
- Georgetown (➤ 18), Lincoln Memorial (➤ 28)
- Free 1-hour tours between 10AM and 1PM. Free Millennium Stage performance daily at 6PM

Matisse tapestry

Lincoln Memorial

HIGHLIGHTS

- Daniel Chester French's *Lincoln*
- Inscription of Lincoln's 1863 Gettysburg Address and Second Inaugural Address
- Reflecting pool
- View

INFORMATION

- E5, locator map B3
- 23rd Street NW
- 202/426-6841, www.nps.gov/linc/home.htm
- 8AM–midnight
- Free
- Excellent
- Foggy Bottom
- Vietnam Veterans Memorial (➤ 30), F. D. R. & Jefferson Memorials (➤ 34), Korean War Memorial (➤ 59)
- Tours on request

So powerful and sombre is this memorial that you can easily imagine Lincoln rising up and resuming his epic struggles. The view from the steps at sunset is one of the city's most romantic, with the Washington Monument reflected in the rectangular pool at its base.

Tribute John Wilkes Booth shot Abraham Lincoln in Ford's Theater on 14 April 1865. Lincoln died the next day. Four decades passed before congressional and public support reached a consensus on the design and siting of a monument to this well-loved president. Work began on the memorial on the eve of World War I and continued until 1922, when Henry Bacon's Greek temple was dedicated.

History in stone The 36 columns symbolize the 36 states in the Union when Lincoln died. The names of the 48 states in the Union, at the time of the monument's dedication, are inscribed above the parapet's crowning frieze. The 5.8m (19ft) marble statue by Daniel Chester French captures a contemplative Lincoln. The monument's construction is chronicled in a small museum on the lower level. Lincoln's Gettysburg Address and his Second Inaugural Address are inscribed on the south and north walls. It was here on the steps, a century after Lincoln emancipated the slaves, that Martin Luther King, Jr., delivered his famous "I Have a Dream" speech before a crowd of 200,000 people.

The colonnaded facade of the Lincoln Memorial

Phillips Collection

Washington's distinguished museums include the first permanent modern art museum in the US. The Phillips Collection comprises more than 25,000 works, of which between 250 and 300 are on exhibit at any one time in this intimate gallery.

Unique collection In 1921 Duncan Phillips opened two gallery rooms in his Georgian-revival mansion as a memorial to his father and brother. In the same year he married painter Marjorie Acker. Together they assembled an unparalleled collection of French Impressionists—including Auguste Renoir's *Luncheon of the Boating Party*, acquired in 1923 for the then record price of $125,000—Post-Impressionists, cubists, 17th- and 18th-century masters, and American modernists. They avoided the ordinary and sought out paintings that glowed with an artist's unique vision; their unerring eye has given the collection a special quality. The enlarged but still intimate Goh annex, which opened in 1989, provides additional space for travelling exhibitions and for exhibitions of the permanent collection, which change periodically.

Masterpieces The playful Swiss painter Paul Klee is well represented here, as is the master of brilliant domestic images, Pierre Bonnard. Americans Arthur Dove, Georgia O'Keeffe, and Mark Rothko coexist peacefully alongside Pablo Picasso, Claude Monet, and Edgar Degas. The Music Room on the first floor, with its oak paneling and wainscoting, displays works by one of Phillips's favorite artists, cubist Georges Braque. The paintings are hung throughout the house, and art students, who serve as wardens, are always willing to discuss works in detail.

HIGHLIGHTS

- *Luncheon of the Boating Party*, Auguste Renoir
- *The Way to the Citadel*, Paul Klee
- *Repentant Peter*, El Greco
- *Entrance to the Public Garden at Arles*, Vincent van Gogh
- *Dancers at the Bar*, Edgar Degas
- American modernists
- *The Terrace*, Pierre Bonnard

INFORMATION

- F3, locator map B1
- 1600–1612 21st Street NW
- 202/387-2151, www.phillipscollection.org/
- Tue–Sat 10–5 (Thu 5–9); Sun 12–7
- Moderate Sat, Sun; contributions Mon–Fri
- Excellent
- Café
- Dupont Circle
- John F. Kennedy Center (➤ 27), National Geographic Society (➤ 31)
- Tours Wed and Sat 2PM. Concerts in the Music Room Sep–May: Sun 5PM

Luncheon of the Boating Party, *Pierre Auguste Renoir (1881)*

Vietnam Veterans Memorial

HIGHLIGHTS

- Inscribed names
- Frederick Hart's sculptural group
- Glenna Goodacre's sculptural group
- The city reflected in the polished stone

INFORMATION

- E5, locator map B3
- Near Constitution Avenue between 21st and 22nd Streets NW
- 202/634-1568, www.nps.gov/vive/home.htm
- 24 hours; staffed 8AM–midnight
- Free
- Excellent
- Foggy Bottom
- Presidents' monuments (➤ 28, 33, 34); Einstein Memorial (➤ 59); Korean War Memorial (➤ 59)
- Rangers available to assist in locating names

Names on the Wall

This starkly simple sculpture has been called the most moving memorial in Washington, and on most days there is an almost constant procession of hushed visitors moving down into what one veteran has called the "black gash of shame."

Simple reminder Yale University student Maya Ying Lin was only 21 when she won the national design competition with a memorial that is simplicity itself—two triangular black granite walls, each 75m (246ft) long, set at a 125-degree angle and pointing towards the Washington Monument and Lincoln Memorial. At its apex, the walls rise to 3m (10ft) and seem to overpower those who stand beneath them. The names of heroes who made the ultimate sacrifice for their country are placed chronologically: Between 1959 and 1975 more than 58,000 were killed or reported missing in action. It was the longest armed war in American history.

A place to reflect The polished surface reflects sky, trees, nearby monuments, and the faces of visitors searching for the names of fathers, sons, and loved ones. Each day National Park Service Rangers collect mementoes left near soldiers' names: letters, uniforms, military emblems, photographs. These tokens receive the care of museum acquisitions and are held in perpetuity as part of the history of the nation. Initially, some veterans thought the Wall insufficient to represent them. So in 1984 Frederick Hart's slightly larger-than-life sculpture of three soldiers was dedicated, sited at one of the entrances to the Wall. The Vietnam Women's Memorial, a sculpture by Glenna Goodacre, was dedicated nearby on Veterans' Day in 1993.

National Geographic Society

Gilbert Hovey Grosvenor, who founded the National Geographic magazine in 1888, brought geography alive for his readers by his use of stunning photography, and the Society continues this tradition of breathing life into a subject in its splendid exhibits.

Architectural history Since 1888 the Society has increased and diffused geographic knowledge as directed by its charter, in part via the familiar yellow monthly *National Geographic* magazine. The National Geo buildings—1902 Beaux Arts original, 1964 Edward Durrell Stone's dominant 10-story tower, and the 1984 Skidmore, Owings and Merrill angular terraced ziggurat—create an enclave of 20th-century American architecture.

Living world Explorers Hall is on the first floor of the society's glass-and-marble building which was designed by Kennedy Center architect Edward Durrell Stone. *Geographica*, a high-tech, celebratory exhibit installed for the magazine's centennial in 1988, lets you touch a tornado, explore a Martian landscape, test your knowledge of early human development, investigate undersea archaeology, and learn trivia about space. Here, too, is the world's largest freestanding globe, 10.4m (34ft) in circumference, which shows earth at a scale of 1 inch to 60 miles. There are also short films, and an interactive amphitheatre called Earth Station One, that simulates orbital flight and looks at earth from out in space. Stunning images taken by the Society's legendary photographers enhance every exhibition. The gift shop sells Society maps, books, videos, and CD-ROMs.

HIGHLIGHTS

- World's largest freestanding globe
- Touch a tornado
- Earth Station One
- Holographic images
- Model of Jacques Cousteau's diving saucer
- Moon rock

INFORMATION

- F3, locator map C2
- 17th and M Streets NW
- 202/857-7588, www.nationalgeographic.com/
- Mon–Sat 9–5; Sun 10–5
- Free
- Excellent
- Dupont Circle, Farragut North
- Dupont Circle (➤ 17)
- Tue noon: free showings of National Geographic specials in the TV room

Top **25**

7

The White House

HIGHLIGHTS

- *Abraham Lincoln*, G. P. A. Healy
- Jacqueline Kennedy Rose Garden
- French and English gilded silver
- East Room
- *George Washington*, Gilbert Stuart

INFORMATION

- F4, locator map C2
- 1600 Pennsylvania Avenue
- 202/456-7041, www.whitehouse.gov/
- Tue–Sat 10–noon
- Free
- Excellent
- McPherson Square, Metro Center
- Washington Monument (➤ 33)
- For free timed tickets and historical exhibits, go to the White House Visitors Center, 15th and E Streets NW Daily 7.30–4. During busy seasons the queue begins to form at 6AM. American citizens can contact their congressmen for advance tickets

In this the city's oldest public building, virtually every desk, every sterling tea service, every silver platter, decanter, painting, and floor covering intertwines with the historic events of the American democracy.

History Despite the fact that Thomas Jefferson thought James Hogan's original design "big enough for two emperors, one Pope, and the grand Lama" when he became the second occupant of 1600 Pennsylvania Avenue in 1801, the third President built additional wings to house domestic quarters for the president and offices. Today the White House looks modest, flanked as it is by the US Treasury, the largest Greek-revival building in the world, and the Old Executive Office Building. The British burned the White House in 1814, and the rebuilding that followed was only one of several renovations conducted over the years.

Works of art The president's house holds an impressive display of decorative arts from the Sheraton, French and American Empire, Queen Anne, and Federal periods. There are carved Carrara marble mantels, Bohemian cut-glass chandeliers, Turkish Hereke carpets, and elaborate plasterwork throughout, as well as the gardens. The exact tour may vary depending on official functions, but usually open are the ceremonial East Room, with Gilbert Stuart's 1797 portrait of George Washington, the Vermeil Room containing 17th- to early 20th-century French and English gilded silver (vermeil), the small drawing room known as the Green Room, the neoclassical State Dining Room where George P. A. Healy's Abraham Lincoln portrait hangs, and the Blue and Red Rooms, known for their superb French Empire furnishings.

Washington Monument

An icon of Washington life, this monolith is the world's tallest masonry structure. The 70-second ride to the pinnacle is rewarded by a marvellous panorama across DC, as well as over Maryland, and Virginia.

Money The Washington Monument, which punctuates the axis of the White House and Jefferson Memorial, and the US Congress and Lincoln Memorial, perfectly exemplifies how government projects can go awry. A 1783 Congressional resolution called for an equestrian statue to honor George Washington for his heroic leadership during the American Revolution. Nothing happened until 1836, when private citizens formed the Washington National Monument Society and solicited one dollar from every living American. When they had raised $28,000, the group laid the cornerstone to Robert Mills' design in 1848. The Civil War interrupted work on the obelisk; construction did not resume until 1876, sparked by the national fervor surrounding the centennial of the American Revolution. Note how the colour of the marble changes 45.7m (150ft) up.

View The views from the top of the 169m (555ft) marble obelisk cover most of DC and parts of Maryland and Virginia: look for the Tidal Basin, the Jefferson and Lincoln memorials, the White House, the US Capitol, the Library of Congress, and the Smithsonian Institution. If you take the weekend guided walk down the monument's 898 steps you will see the commemorative plaques donated during building by states, masonic lodges, church groups, and foreign countries. An observation deck at 152m (500ft) above the ground was opened in 2002.

HIGHLIGHTS

- Views from the top
- Exhibit in base

INFORMATION

- F5–G5, locator map C3
- The Mall at 15th Street NW
- 202/426-6840, www.nps.gov/wamo/home.htm
- Apr–Labor Day: daily 8AM–midnight. Labor Day–Mar: daily 9–5.
- Free
- Excellent
- Smithsonian
- Timed tickets distributed daily at 8.30AM at the site and through Ticketmaster 202/432-7328. Tours Sat, Sun 10, 2. Queues are shorter at night

F. D. R. & Jefferson Memorials

HIGHLIGHTS

- Jefferson bronze
- Inscribed Declaration of Independence

INFORMATION

Jefferson Memorial
- F6, locator map C3
- Tidal Basin, south bank
- 202/426-6821, www.nps.gov/thje/home.htm
- Daily 8AM–midnight
- Free
- Excellent
- Smithsonian, then 20-minute walk

F. D. R. Memorial
- F6
- West Potomac Park
- 202/228-2491
- Daylight hours
- Free
- Smithsonian, then 30-minute walk

The Jefferson bronze

The Jefferson Memorial was dedicated by President Franklin Delano Roosevelt on the 200th anniversary of Jefferson's birth, 13 April 1943. Roosevelt's own memorial consisting of ten bronze sculptures was created nearby and dedicated in 1997.

Classical The Jefferson Memorial forms a north–south axis with the White House. Architect John Russell Pope adapted Rome's Pantheon in deference to Jefferson's love for classical architecture. Jefferson, an amateur architect himself, had used similar circular domed structures at his home, Monticello, and at the University of Virginia. However, some critics derided Pope's design as old-fashioned, while others argued that Jefferson's philosophy dictated a more utilitarian structure. Eventually, the Pope memorial was dedicated in 1943.

Sculpture A wide plaza overlooks the Tidal Basin with its cherry trees, and stairs lead up through a portico, surrounded by a colonnade encircling an open centre. The pediment supports marble figures of Jefferson, Benjamin Franklin, John Adams, Roger Sherman, and Robert Livingston, members of the committee that drafted the Declaration of Independence. Rudolph Evans produced the central 5.8m (19ft) bronze of Jefferson, and excerpts of his speeches and writings are carved into the walls. The sculptures at the F. D. R. Memorial nearby depict Franklin Delano and Eleanor Roosevelt and events from the Great Depression and World War II.

US Holocaust Memorial Museum

This memorial to the 6 million people killed by the Nazis between 1933 and 1945 graphically portrays both the personal stories and the wider issues of persecution and human tragedy. The museum sets new standards for design and historical interpretation.

Disturbing "You cannot deal with the Holocaust as a reasonable thing," explained architect James Ingo Freed. To that end, he created a discordant building, intended to disturb the classical and sometimes placid facades elsewhere in Washington. There are stunning high-tech audiovisuals, and computer technology documents and links survivors worldwide.

Nightmare Watchtowers line the north and south walls, contributing to the prison-like atmosphere that prevails in the central atrium, the Hall of Witness, via exposed beams, metal railings, and malevolent elevators. A memory or a nightmare lurks everywhere you look or stand. The story told here is not of war but of humanity gone berserk. In so far as is possible, victims and survivors relate their experiences directly. You will find yourself horrified and shocked but compelled to continue, and grateful when provided with a place to rest and reflect. The Hall of Remembrance on the second floor provides just such a space, its filtered light and soaring stonework providing spiritual solace. A special exhibit for children under 12, *Daniel's Story*, re-creates what life was like for a young boy trapped in the downward spiral of Nazi occupation. The implicit question posed by the museum—the challenge of the visit—is not "Why did it happen?" but "How do we prevent similar occurrences?"

HIGHLIGHTS

- Hall of Witness
- Hall of Remembrance
- For children (8–12): *Daniel's Story*

INFORMATION

- G5, locator map D3
- 14th Street and Wallenberg Place SW, south of Independence Avenue
- www.ushmm.org/
- Daily 10–5.30. Closed Yom Kippur
- Free
- Excellent
- Kosher restaurant
- Smithsonian
- Presidents' memorials (➤ 28, 33, 34), Bureau of Engraving and Printing (➤ 37), Smithsonian Institution (➤ 39)
- Timed tickets distributed daily at 10AM; queue early (before 9AM) or book two weeks in advance. Advance tickets through Protix ☎ 800/400-9373

National Museum of American History

HIGHLIGHTS

- The *Star Spangled Banner*
- Hands-on-History Room
- Hands-on-Science Room
- *John Bull*
- Ruby slippers from the *Wizard of Oz*

INFORMATION

- G5, locator map D3
- Constitution Avenue and 14th Street NW
- 202/357-2700, americanhistory.si.edu/
- Daily 10–5.30
- Free
- Cafeteria
- Excellent
- Smithsonian, Federal Triangle
- US Holocaust Memorial Museum (➤ 35), Bureau of Engraving and Printing (➤ 37), Smithsonian Institution (➤ 39)
- Tours available

From the manuscript for the *Star Spangled Banner* and Judy Garland's ruby slippers to Duke Ellington's papers and inaugural ballgowns of the First Ladies—here are the objects that tell the story of the US.

All-American Displays depict events and themes that define American life, such as "Field to Factory," recounting how African-Americans migrated from the agricultural South to industrial cities of the North. "A More Perfect Union" contributes to the dialogue about the US Constitution, depicting the withdrawal of civil liberties from Japanese-Americans during World War II. The largest exhibition, "The Information Age," showcases automated gear ranging from early telephones to robotics to high-definition television. "From Parlor to Politics" and "First Ladies: Political Role and Public Image" depict women's political impact. An exhibition on time marks the millennium, while expansive displays on the Industrial Revolution and "Science in American Life" round out the offerings. Mail postcards from an original West Virginia general store; get your picture taken in front of the steam engine *John Bull*, the country's oldest working locomotive; and, as an all-American finale, have an old-fashioned root beer float in the museum's ice-cream parlour.

George Washington as a Greek god

Bureau of Engraving & Printing

Usually when visiting a new city you don't make a beeline for a nondescript government building. But here children and adults alike delight in watching powerful printing presses turn out more than $20 million every day.

Dollar bills It was in 1914 that the Bureau moved to this site from the redbrick Auditor's Building on a nearby corner. Today, all US currency, stamps, presidential invitations, and military certificates are printed on the site. Federal presses produce a staggering $100 billion (US) annually, nearly all of which replaces currency already in circulation, in addition to 30 billion (US) postage stamps. Even slightly imperfect bills are summarily shredded. Also here is the grandly titled Office of Mutilated Currency, where citizens go to redeem bills partially destroyed by fire, flood, or laundry.

Printing presses After a film on the history of currency, you file past processing rooms where the bills are produced. The printing room turns out giant sheets of currency, made not from paper but from a cotton/linen fabric, each holding 32 dollar bills, at a rate of 8,000 sheets an hour. The sheets are checked for any imperfections, trimmed, then stacked into bundles or 'bricks' of 4,000 notes ready for distribution to Federal Reserve Banks across the nation. The 35-minute self-guided tour ends at an exhibition hall filled with informative displays on the history of currency, counterfeiting, and stamps. Do not be daunted by the queues: They move rapidly. Outside, you'll find yourself near the Tidal Basin, one of the most beautiful spots in the city. Here you can rent a paddle boat and take a leisurely stroll along pathways lined with cherry trees—gorgeously pink in early spring.

HIGHLIGHTS

- Presses printing dollars
- Stacks of money, bundled for shipping
- Film on the history of currency
- Exhibition on stamps
- View of the Tidal Basin

INFORMATION

- G6, locator map D3
- 14 and C Streets SW
- 202/874-3019, www.bep.treas.gov/
- Sep–May: Mon–Fri 9–2. Jun–Aug: Mon–Fri 9–2, 5–6.40
- Smithsonian
- Excellent
- Free
- US Holocaust Memorial Museum (➤ 35)
- Self-guided tours. Tickets and advance reservations required Apr–Sep 202/874-2330

Freer & Arthur M. Sackler Galleries

HIGHLIGHTS

The Freer Gallery of Art

- *Peacock Room*, James McNeill Whistler
- *Princess from the Land of Porcelain*, James McNeill Whistler
- Ancient Chinese artefacts
- Korean ceramics
- Japanese painted screens

The Arthur M. Sackler Gallery

- Chinese jades and bronzes
- Islamic manuscripts
- Ancient Iranian metalworks

INFORMATION

- G5, locator map D3
- 12th Street and Jefferson Drive or Independence Avenue, SW
- 202/357-2700, www.asia.si.edu/
- Daily 10–5
- Free
- Excellent
- Smithsonian
- National Air and Space Museum (➤ 43), Hirshhorn Sculpture Garden (➤ 59)
- Tours Thu–Tue 11.30AM

Top: inside the Peacock Room, *Freer Gallery*
Right: James McNeill Whistler

One of the little-known treasures in the city, the Freer contains over 26,000 works of Asian art as well as one of the world's largest collections of paintings by James McNeill Whistler. The Asian art collection is complemented by exhibitions from all over the world.

Freer Gallery of Art Charles A. Platt designed this granite palazzo-style building in 1923, which was renovated between 1988 and 1993. You can see Asian porcelains, Japanese screens, Chinese painting and bronzes, Korean stone-ware, and Islamic art. James McNeill Whistler's blue and gold *Peacock Room* was inspired by the bird's striking plumage. It was decorated in 1876 for a London town house, and purchased by Freer, a friend of Whistler, in 1904.

Arthur M. Sackler Gallery You can reach the Sackler Gallery by walking through an underground passage from the Freer or from Independence Avenue via a 1987 granite pavilion by Shepley Bullfinch Richardson and Abbott. Yes, the museum is underground (as is the National Museum of African Art across the plaza) but don't let that keep you away. A series of bridges and light wells alleviate any tomb-like aura and allow you to see the Islamic, Iranian, and Chinese material from unexpected and unusual viewpoints.

Top **25**

14

Smithsonian Institution

Tourists pouring off Metro escalators on summer mornings often ask commuters, "Where's the Smithsonian?" There is usually a suspicious silence on the visitor's part when the local answers, "Everything you see is the Smithsonian."

Benefactor An Englishman, James Smithson, stipulated that his estate should go "to the United States of America, to found at Washington, under the name of the Smithsonian Institution, an Establishment for the increase and diffusion of knowledge." After typical political wrangling, John Quincy Adams convinced Congress to take the gift, which was worth about $515,000 when it was accepted in 1846. Today the Smithsonian Institution comprises the largest cluster of museums in the world, as well as the National Zoo, and holds 140 million objects and specimens, with countless research projects worldwide on topics ranging from Russian voles and Native American baskets, to endangered insects of the rain forests, aerodynamics, and molecular biology. The Smithsonian has 6,000 employees and an annual budget of nearly $400 million.

Castle Start your visit at James Renwick's iconic 1855 turreted, asymmetrical, red-sandstone castle—the Smithsonian's headquarters. The Crypt in the north foyer contains the body of James Smithson, moved here in 1904, while the statue at the entrance is of the Smithsonian's first secretary, physicist Joseph Henry. The castle contains a state-of-the-art information centre full of interactive maps, touch-screen programs, and brochures. Guides help you plan your visit to the Smithsonian and other Washington sights.

HIGHLIGHTS

Mall Museums

- Arts and Industries Building
- Freer & Arthur M. Sackler Galleries (➤ 38)
- Hirshorn Sculpture Garden (➤ 59)
- National Air & Space Museum (➤ 43)
- National Gallery of Art (➤ 42)
- National Museum of African Art
- National Museum of American History (➤ 36)
- National Museum of Natural History (➤ 54)

Museums off the Mall

- Anacostia Museum (➤ 52)
- National Postal Museum
- National Zoological Park (➤ 55)
- Renwick Gallery

INFORMATION

- G5–H5, locator map D3
- Jefferson Drive at 10th Street SW
- 202/357-2700, www.si.edu/
- Daily 10–5.30
- Free
- Excellent
- The Commons for Smithsonian members
- Smithsonian
- Film every 20 minutes

FBI Building

HIGHLIGHTS

- Live-ammo demonstration
- FBI Most Wanted files
- FBI Most Famous Cases
- Exhibition of FBI History
- Fingerprint matching

INFORMATION

- G5, locator map D2
- E and 9th Streets NW
- 202/324-3447, www.fbi.gov/
- Mon–Fri 8.45–4.15
- Free
- Excellent
- Federal Triangle
- Smithsonian Institution (➤ 39), Ford's Theater (➤ 82)
- Tour every 20 minutes

FBI crest

Few subjects fascinate law-abiding Americans more than crime and crime prevention. It's not surprising, therefore, that for many visitors the FBI building is on their list of "ten most wanted" things to do in Washington.

Big Brother Stanley Gladych's modern, concrete building—a 1974 example of brutalist architecture—conjures a Big Brother on Pennsylvania Avenue, halfway between the Capitol and the White House. About 8,000 federal employees operate out of this looming structure, which fills an entire city block and embodies the "idea of a central core of files." Chartered in 1908, the FBI is the supreme federal authority on domestic crime. It deals with terrorism, organized crime, and industrial espionage, among other matters. Even today, the FBI's values are those of its most famous director, J. Edgar Hoover, who ran the agency from 1928 to 1972, an astounding 44 years. The FBI is the most respected investigative force in the US, and its headquarters is one of the most popular tourist attractions in Washington. Be prepared for queues.

Wanted The tour takes in historical exhibits about famous cases the FBI has solved, an introduction to laboratory work, including DNA analysis of hair fibres and blood samples, fingerprint matching, and a live-ammunition firearms demonstration, followed by a question and answer session. Be alert when you visit: Two of the FBI's most-wanted characters were fingered by tourists who saw the "Wanted" posters on the tour.

National Archives

Walk through the building's colossal bronze entrance doors, up the sweeping staircase, and witness the US through official archives: the Charters of Freedom, the gun that shot JFK, the Watergate tapes—it's all here.

Millions of documents John Russell Pope's Beaux Arts building has served as the repository for all the nation's valuable official records since 1935. At last count it contained 3.2 billion (US) textual documents, 1.6 million maps, 14.9 million photographs, and enough film and videotapes to encircle the globe many times.

Charters of Freedom After passing through a metal detector you are led toward a throne-like structure in a domed rotunda with a Corinthian portico. Raised and enshrined at the centre of the structure are the Declaration of Independence, the Constitution, and the Bill of Rights, sealed in bronze helium-filled cases covered with green ultraviolet filters. Closed for renovation in 2001, the exhibit halls are due to reopen in 2003 at which time the Charters of Freedom, as they are called, will be easily seen by visitors via air-tight cases that allow more pages of the documents to be displayed along with interactive exhibits featuring these essential documents. At the end of each day, after all the visitors and researchers have gone home, the security staff lower the throne and the Charters into a bomb-proof vault beneath the exhibition floor. Also on display are murals by Barry Faulkner entitled *The Declaration of Independence* and *The Constitution*. Changing exhibitions highlight the material—letters, photographs, and posters—from the vast collections maintained by the Archives.

HIGHLIGHTS

- Charters of Freedom
- Murals by Barry Faulkner
- Changing exhibition gallery

INFORMATION

- H5, locator map E2
- Constitution Avenue at 7th Street NW
- 202/501-5205, www.archives.gov/
- Daily 10–5.30
- Free
- Excellent
- Archives
- Smithsonian Institution (➤ 39), US Botanic Gardens (➤ 44), US Capitol (➤ 45)
- Tours daily 10.15, 1.15 (reservations required)

Top **25**

17

National Gallery of Art

HIGHLIGHTS

- East Wing
- *Venus and Adonis*, Titian
- *The Alba Madonna*, Raphael
- *Laocoön*, El Greco
- *Daniel in the Lion's Den*, Peter Paul Rubens
- *Woman Holding a Balance*, Johannes Vermeer
- *A Girl with a Watering Can*, Auguste Renoir
- *Woman with a Parasol–Madame Monet and her Son*, Claude Monet
- *The Skater*, Gilbert Stuart

INFORMATION

- H5, locator map E3
- Madison Drive between 3rd and 7th Streets NW
- 202/737-4215, www.nga.gov/
- Mon–Sat 10–5; Sun 11–6
- Free
- Excellent
- Concourse Buffet, Cascade Café, Garden Café
- Archives
- National Air and Space Museum (➤ 43), US Botanic Gardens (➤ 44), US Capitol (➤ 45)
- Tours daily

Here you can see the US's only Leonardo da Vinci painting, *Ginevra,* along with the world's top travelling exhibitions. Every American owns an equal share of the art here, which may well prompt a burst of patriotic pride.

Vision When Andrew Mellon was secretary of the treasury (1921–32) he realized that the capital city lacked a great gallery illustrating the development of Western art. So when he died in 1937 he left an endowment and his renowned collection of paintings and sculpture to the American people, and passed on his dream to his son. Paul Mellon oversaw the construction of John Russell Pope's classical building, opened in 1941, and eventually of I. M. Pei's stunning East Wing, opened in 1978, perhaps the finest modern building in the US.

Western art The permanent collection includes Renaissance painting, with works by Italian masters Raphael and Titian, Spanish painters Velasquez, El Greco, and Goya, as well as Flemish, German, and Dutch paintings from van der Weyden and Dürer to Rubens and Vermeer. The French are well represented by Watteau, Corot, Manet, Renoir, and all the Impressionists. Works by William Hogarth begin the tour of British painting, from Gainsborough to Turner. American painting is represented by Gilbert Stuart, Winslow Homer, James McNeill Whistler, and others. Also on offer are films and lectures about the works of art, while you can access information about the museum's paintings in the Micro Gallery's user-friendly computerized collection. Outside, a sculpture garden, opened in 1999, includes works by Roy Lichtenstein and Claes Oldenburg, and a huge bronze spider by Louise Bourgeois.

National Air & Space Museum

The most visited museum in the world takes parents and children alike on a pioneering journey from the first manned motorized flight to the most recent space exploration—"infinity and beyond!"

Flight pioneers This museum was the Smithsonian's bicentennial gift to the nation. More than 10 million visitors a year explore its monumental glass and granite galleries. The collection—begun as early as 1861, when the first secretary of the Smithsonian urged experiments in balloon flight—includes the Wright Brothers' 1903 *Flyer;* Charles Lindbergh's *Spirit of St. Louis;* Chuck Yeager's *Bell X-1*, in which he broke the sound barrier; and *The Voyager*, in which Dick Rutan and Jeana Yeager flew nonstop around the world.

Into space Among the spectacular rockets, missiles, and space vehicles in the Space Halls you can see the Columbia Space Shuttle, the Apollo-Soyuz spacecraft, Skylab, and lunar exploration vehicles. The Steven F. Udvar-Hazy Center, a new display, is due to open at Dulles International Airport in December 2003.

HIGHLIGHTS

- Wright brothers' 1903 *Flyer*
- Charles Lindbergh's *Spirit of St. Louis*
- Chuck Yeager's *Bell X-1 Glamorous Glennis*
- Soviet *Sputnik*
- John Glenn's *Friendship* and *Apollo 11*
- Columbia Space Shuttle
- Skylab
- Lunar Exploration Vehicles

INFORMATION

- H5, locator map E3
- Independence Avenue at 6th Street SW
- 202/357-2700, www.nasm.si.edu/
- Daily 10–5.30
- Free. Einstein Planetarium: moderate
- Excellent
- Wright Place Cafeteria
- L'Enfant Plaza
- National Gallery of Art (➤ 42), US Botanic Gardens (➤ 44)
- Langley Theatre, IMAX: films every 35 minutes

Spirit of St. Louis, flown by Charles Lindbergh

US Botanic Gardens

HIGHLIGHTS

- Seasonal displays
- Orchids and tropical plants
- Coffee, chocolate, and banyan trees
- Bartholdi Fountain

INFORMATION

- H5, locator map E3
- 1st Street SW and Maryland Avenue
- 202/225-7099, www.usbg.gov/
- Daily 9–5. Under renovation at press time; call before you visit
- Free
- Excellent
- Federal Center SW
- Smithsonian Institution (➤ 39), US Capitol (➤ 45)

December's poinsettia display is an annual must for Washingtonians. If you visit on a weekday morning in winter, when you may well be alone in the desert display, you can easily imagine yourself in Arizona or the Sahara.

Exotic glasshouse US explorers in the 19th century needed a place to conserve the specimens they brought home from the South Seas, so Congress authorized the first greenhouse in 1842. The present 3,716sq-m (40,000sq-ft) conservatory, an attractive combination of iron-and-glass greenhouse and stone orangeries, at the southwestern corner of Capitol Hill, was erected in 1931. Following a four-year $33.5 million renovation, the Gardens are now home to more than 4,000 plants.

Flowers for all seasons The main entrance hall serves as a seasonal gallery displaying by turns Christmas poinsettias, tulips and hyacinths, or chrysanthemums. Not far away there is a permanent planting of high desert flora as well as a steamy tropical exhibit in the large glass pavilion. In two smaller conservatories you can see orchids, as well as coffee, chocolate, and banyan trees, and plants resembling those on earth during the Jurassic period 200 million years ago. If you can ignore traffic whizzing by, you'll appreciate the tiny pocket park across Independence Avenue—it is arguably the most beautiful in the city. Here, plantings frame and showcase the cast-iron Bartholdi Fountain (1876), embellished with sea nymphs, monsters, tritons, and lighted globes. It was designed by Frédéric-Auguste Bartholdi, best known as the sculptor of the Statue of Liberty, for the Philadelphia Centennial Exhibition, intending it to represent the elements of light and water.

US Capitol

Imitated on state buildings throughout the country, the dome makes an iconic backdrop for television newscasters and politicians who want to associate their pronouncements with a symbol of American democracy.

Icon The dome was an engineering feat when undertaken in 1851 by Capitol architect Charles Walter and US Army Quartermaster General Montgomery Meigs. It became a political symbol before it was half finished: The Civil War broke out while it was under construction, and the Capitol housed the wounded and their caregivers. Many advised President Lincoln to halt work on the building, but he was adamant that progress continue as "a sign we intend the Union shall go on." The cast-iron dome, rising 85.3m (280ft), was completed in 1863.

Founding Fathers You can wait in the Great Rotunda for a guided tour, or wander freely in the public spaces. The paintings overhead were done from life and from memory by George Washington's aide, John Trumbull. *The Apotheosis of Washington*, a fresco by Constantino Brumidi, depicts classical deities and the Founding Fathers. Brumidi, it was said, consorted with "ladies of the night," whose likenesses then appeared as ample maidens ministering to George Washington. When Congress is in session, you may visit the House or Senate chambers.

HIGHLIGHTS

- Rotunda
- Frescoes by Constantino Brumidi
- Paintings by John Trumbull
- Visit to the House or Senate Chambers

INFORMATION

- J5, locator map F3
- 1st Street between Independence and Constitution Avenues
- 202/225-6827, www.aoc.gov/
- Mon–Sat 9–4.30
- Free
- Excellent
- Capitol Cafeteria, Dining Room
- Capitol South
- US Botanic Gardens (➤ 44), Union Station (➤ 46), US Supreme Court Building (➤ 47), Library of Congress (➤ 48)
- Tours daily, every 30 minutes. A pass to observe a session of Congress can be obtained from a senator's or representative's office by US nationals. Foreign visitors apply at the ground-floor appointment desk. When Congress works overtime, the exterior dome light in the cupola is lit.

The dome's colonnade

Top **25**

21

Union Station

HIGHLIGHTS

- Main Hall
- Statues of Roman legionnaires
- East Hall
- Presidential Waiting Room
- Columbus Plaza

INFORMATION

- J4, locator map F2
- 50 Massachusetts Avenue NE
- 202/371-9441, www.unionstationdc.com/
- 24 hours for train service; stores, restaurants, and theatres vary
- Free
- Excellent
- Many
- Union Station
- US Capitol (➤ 45)

The lovely Union Station houses shops, restaurants, and a cinema, as well as the railway, and is used by all: movie-going teenagers, office workers doing errands at lunch, dining dealmakers, commuting bureaucrats, and tourists.

World's largest Architect Daniel H. Burnham lived up to his motto, "Make No Little Plans," when he undertook the consolidation of DC's several train lines early last century. Burnham's vaulted, white-marble, Beaux Arts Union Station was the largest train station in the world when it opened in 1907. Today, it is one of the most visited spots in Washington, the destination for up to 23 million people each year. Renovated and reopened in 1988, it now houses a huge variety of restaurants and boutiques. There are nine movie screens, and it is both an active train terminal and a Metro stop.

More than trains Inside, thousands of travellers pass under a cavernous 29m (96ft) high coffered ceiling, embellished with gold leaf and guarded by 46 Augustus Saint-Gaudens statues of Roman legionnaires. The original Presidential Waiting Room is now a restaurant. The market-like East Hall has stalls selling items from around the world. Outside, a grand memorial to Christopher Columbus by Lorado Taft fronts the massive Doric colonnade, and allegorical neoclassical sculptures depicting fire, electricity, and mechanics set off the skyline. You can visit another restored Burnham building to the right, the Old Post Office, which now houses the Smithsonian Postal Museum. To the left, you can see an example of contemporary Beaux Arts styling in the architect Edward Larrabee Barnes's new Thurgood Marshall Federal Judicial Center.

US Supreme Court Building

One justice called this 1935 neoclassical building, designed by Cass Gilbert, Jr., in gleaming Vermont marble, "bombastically pretentious...for a quiet group of old boys such as the Supreme Court."

Judgments Since the arrival of justices Sandra Day O'Conner and Ruth Bader Ginsburg, the Court is no longer an old-boys' stronghold, though it has never really been quiet. The 1857 Dred Scott decision, which held that Congress had no authority to limit slavery, contributed to the onset of the Civil War. Rulings on abortion have frequently made the plaza in front of the building, one of Washington's most impressive Greek temples, a focus of civil disobedience. *Brown v. Board of Education* required the integration of schools and bus travel across the land, and *Engel v. Vitale* outlawed school prayer. But in another way, the Court works quietly. Justices are appointed for life and rarely give interviews. The Court is not televised, and information never leaks out of the building, as is common elsewhere in the city.

Law in action The steps up to the colonnaded entrance are flanked by two white marble allegorical figures by James Earle Fraser, depicting *The Contemplation of Justice* and *The Authority of Law*. The magnificent bronze entrance doors, designed by John Donnely, Jr., lead into the huge entrance hall with busts of all the former chief justices. When the Court is in session you can join the "three-minute line" and glimpse proceedings from the Standing Gallery. A statue of John Marshall, Chief Justice from 1755–1835, dominates the ground floor where a short film and changing exhibits describe the work of the Court.

HIGHLIGHTS

- Bronze entrance doors
- Plaza sculpture
- Busts of chief justices
- Film and exhibits on Court history
- The Court in session

INFORMATION

- J5, locator map F3
- 1st and East Capitol Streets NE
- 202/479-3211, www.supremecourtus.gov/
- Mon–Fri 9–4.30
- Free
- Excellent
- Cafeteria
- Capitol South, Union Station
- US Capitol (➤ 45), Library of Congress (➤ 48)
- Lectures on the half-hour when the Court is not in session

Spring blossom softens the stern facade

Library of Congress

HIGHLIGHTS

- *Torch of Learning* on green copper dome
- Beaux Arts design
- Main Reading Room
- Sculpture inside and out
- View of the Capitol from the Madison Building cafeteria

INFORMATION

- J5, locator map F3
- 1st Street and Independence Avenue SE
- 202/707-5458, www.loc.gov/
- Mon–Sat 10–5
- Free
- Excellent. Visitor Services 202/707-9779 provides American Sign Language interpretation
- Cafeteria, coffee shop, Montpelier Restaurant
- Capitol South
- US Capitol (➤ 45), US Supreme Court Building (➤ 47)
- Tours begin at the Jefferson Building Mon–Sat 11, 1, 2.30, 4. Library resources are open to anyone over 18 pursuing research. Regular changing exhibitions

Libraries and bookstores are one of Washington's big draws. The Library of Congress is the mother lode—it's the world's largest library and the US's national library—with over 115 million items on 965km (600mi) of shelves.

Room to read Congress appropriated funds for a library in 1800. Unfortunately, it was destroyed by the British when they sacked the Capitol in 1814. Thomas Jefferson's personal library then became the nucleus of the new collection. The imposing, granite 1897 Beaux Arts Jefferson Building has a ceremonial Corinthian portico, and sculpted busts of men of letters gazing down. For many scholars, sitting in the Main Reading Room at the mahogany readers' tables 48.8m (160ft) below the domed ceiling is an almost spiritual experience. The art deco Adams Building was completed in 1939, the modern Madison Building opposite in 1980.

Not just books Holdings in the Jefferson, Madison, and Adams buildings, clustered between 1st and 3rd Streets on Pennsylvania Avenue SE, include the contents of Lincoln's pockets on the evening he was shot, original scores by Beethoven and Brahms, props belonging to Houdini, and original drafts of the Declaration of Independence, the Emancipation Proclamation, and the Gettysburg Address. If you have a special interest, a librarian can arrange for you to see relevant artefacts.

The copper dome and Torch of Learning

Shrine of the Immaculate Conception

This is the largest Roman Catholic church in the US and the eighth largest in the world. Renowned for its mosaics, it is dedicated to Christ's mother, Mary, named Patroness of the United States by Pope Pius IX in 1847.

Construction Work began on the grounds of Catholic University in 1920. The ground-level Crypt Church was completed in 1926. After the Great Depression and World War II, construction began again in earnest during 1954, and the Great Upper Church was dedicated on 20 November 1959.

American saint Separating the Crypt Church from the Chapel of Our Lady of Hostyn is a delicate stained-glass screen depicting scenes from the life of Saint John Neumann, the first American person to be admitted to the sainthood. The Byzantine-style dome, 72m (237ft) in height and 33m (108ft) in diameter, is lavishly decorated with symbols of the Virgin Mary picked out in gold leaf and colored majolica tiles. The 100m (329ft) bell tower houses a 56-bell carillon cast in France and supports a 6m (20ft) gilded cross visible in every direction for far around.

Interior Three rose windows embellished with gold and amethyst illuminate the sanctuary, along with ranks of other windows depicting the lives of Mary, the Holy Family, saints, and redeemed sinners. Sculpture includes George Carr's 37.6-tonne (37-ton) marble *Universal Call to Holiness* on the south wall of the Great Upper Church. But the lasting image is of the extraordinary mosaics—expanses of them on ceilings and walls, in the apse and in the chapels—donated by American Catholics.

HIGHLIGHTS

- Ecclesiastical sculpture
- Mosaics

INFORMATION

- Off map, north of K1; off locator map F1
- Michigan Avenue and 4th Street NE
- 202/526-8300, www.nationalshrine.com/
- Apr–Oct: daily 7–7. Nov–Mar: daily 7–6
- Free
- Excellent
- Cafeteria daily 7.30–2
- Brookland
- Tours by appointment, Mon–Sat 9–noon, 1–3; Sun 1.30–3

The Byzantine-style Christ in the dome

25

Cedar Hill

HIGHLIGHTS

- Harriet Beecher Stowe's desk
- Portraits of Elizabeth Cady Stanton and Susan B. Anthony
- View of Washington

INFORMATION

- L8, off locator map F4
- 1411 W Street SE
- 202/426-5961, www.nps.gov/frdo/
- Mid-Apr to mid-Oct: daily 9–5. Mid-Oct to mid-Apr: 9–4
- Inexpensive
- Good
- By Tourmobile (mid-Jun to Labor Day and Feb: daily) 202/554-7950 **By car** 11th Street Bridge to Martin Luther King Avenue, left on W Street
- Hourly tours, daily 9–4. Reservation 800/365-2267

Statue of Frederick Douglass

Built in 1854, the Italianate country house known as Cedar Hill was the last home of abolitionist Frederick Douglass. Decorative arts, libraries, and family mementos provide an intimate look at his life and work.

Slave America's famous abolitionist was born into slavery in Maryland in about 1818, and was separated from his mother at birth. Years later he wrote that he had never seen her in daylight during the 7 years before she died, as she had had to walk to see him, returning between the end of one work day and sun up the next. Douglass, badly treated by a plantation overseer, was apprenticed by his owner as a ship caulker but he ran away, becoming active in the Massachusetts antislavery movement. Douglas published his first autobiography in 1845. He fled to Europe to avoid slave bounty hunters, where British friends bought him his freedom. He lectured and published widely on antislavery topics, became an adviser to President Lincoln, an ambassador to Haiti, and a supporter of women's suffrage. When he moved into Cedar Hill, he was the first black resident of Anacostia, breaking the prohibition against "Irish, Negro, mulatto, or persons of African blood," according to a developer's advert of the day.

Viewpoint Cedar Hill, now the Frederick Douglass National Historic Site, occupies the highest point in Anacostia, with a great view of the Anacostia River and the capital. Among the many artefacts on display inside the house is the desk at which Harriet Beecher Stowe wrote *Uncle Tom's Cabin*. The National Park Service, which manages the house, maintains an information centre and a bookstore specializing in African-American titles.

WASHINGTON's best

African-American Sites *52–53*

For Children *54–55*

Libraries & Archives *56–57*

Gardens & Sculpture *58–59*

Places of Worship *60–61*

Views *62*

African-American Sites

1212 T Street NW, the house where "Duke" Ellington grew up in the early 1900s

BLACK BROADWAY

Since the area was torched in the 1968 riots, sparked by the assasination of Martin Luther King, Jr., U Street NW has been transformed. The reopening in 1994 of the 1,250-seat Lincoln Theater caps the renaissance and the strip once again deserves the appellation "Black Broadway." *Community Rhythms*, the vibrant murals of artist Al Smith, decorate the U Street-Cardozo Metro entrances and depict the area's regeneration.

In the Top 25

CEDAR HILL (➤ 50)
LINCOLN MEMORIAL (➤ 28)

AFRICAN-AMERICAN CIVIL WAR MEMORIAL AND MUSEUM

In a historic Masonic Temple, this museum tells the story of the 209,145 African-Americans who fought to abolish slavery in the American Civil War. Edward Hamilton's bronze memorial was dedicated in 1999.
G2 1000 U Street NW 202/667-2667 Museum daily 9–5. Memorial 24 hours U Street-Cardozo Free

ANACOSTIA MUSEUM AND CENTER FOR AFRICAN-AMERICAN HISTORY AND CULTURE

The museum presents the African-American contribution to the history of the US.
M9 1901 Fort Place SE 202/287-3306 Daily 10–5 Anacostia Free

EDWARD KENNEDY "DUKE" ELLINGTON RESIDENCE

Though born at 1217 22nd Street NW, "Duke" Ellington (1899–1974) grew up on this street and took piano lessons nearby.
G2 1212 T Street NW Not open to the public U Street-Cardozo

FATHER PATRICK FRANCIS HEALY BUILDING, GEORGETOWN UNIVERSITY

This 1879 baronial fantasy honours the first black Catholic priest and bishop in America, who later became president of Georgetown University.
C3 37th and O Streets NW 202/687-5055 24 hours Rosslyn, then bus No. 38B Free

FREDERICK DOUGLASS HOUSE

The first Washington home of one of the country's most celebrated abolitionists, now part of the Smithsonian.
K5 316 A Street NE Not open to the public Capitol South

HOWARD UNIVERSITY

Chartered in 1867 to educate freed men and women, Howard is the alma mater of Thurgood Marshall, associate justice of the Supreme Court. It occupies 89 acres and houses 12,000 students pursuing nearly 200 areas of study. The law school is widely acknowledged as the place where African-Americans learned how to use the legal system to drive the civil rights movement in the 1960s.
H2 2400 6th Street NW 202/806-6100 Mon–Fri 9–5 Shaw-Howard University

INDUSTRIAL BANK OF WASHINGTON

At the beginning of the 20th century white banks accepted deposits from black people but would not make loans to them. So when John L. Lewis opened his bank in 1913, it soon became known as "the wage earners' bank." In 1932 Texan Jesse Mitchell opened Industrial on this site with $200,000; the bank still serves Washington's African-American community.

G2 · 2000 11th Street NW · 202/722-2050 · Mon–Thu 9–3; Fri 9–3, 4.30–6; Sat 9–noon · U Street-Cardozo

LINCOLN PARK

Charlotte Scott, a Virginia woman, contributed the first $5 towards the Emancipation Memorial, which was supported entirely from funds from free blacks. Dedicated on 14 April 1876, it remained the city's only monument to Abraham Lincoln until 1922, when the Lincoln Memorial was dedicated. In 1974 the Emancipation Memorial was turned away from the Capitol to face the new Mary McLeod Bethune Memorial.

K5 · East Capitol Street between 11th and 13th Streets · Eastern Market

TRUE REFORMERS HALL

Architect John A. Lankford's six-story 1903 building housed a variety of black-owned retail stores, offices, and entertainments, and a drill room and armoury for Washington's black National Guard unit. It later housed a popular dance hall, where Duke Ellington (➤ 50) performed with his band, Duke's Serenaders.

G2 · 1200 U Street NW · Not open to the public · U Street-Cardozo

NATIONAL COUNCIL OF NEGRO WOMEN

The Mary McLeod Bethune Museum and Archives (➤ 56) house the records of the National Council of Negro Women, founded in 1935 and uniting the considerable influence of hundreds of African-American women's groups. These women shaped public policy regarding civil rights, health care, housing, and employment, extending even to the formation of the United Nations.

Mary McLeod Bethune Memorial, Lincoln Park

For Children

INFORMATION SOURCES

The Washington Post "Carousel Weekend" lists local events for children. WKDL radio (1050 AM) caters to children and their parents and often reports on children's events.

The National Museum of American History

In the Top 25

BUREAU OF ENGRAVING & PRINTING (► 37)
FBI BUILDING (► 40)
NATIONAL GEOGRAPHIC SOCIETY, EXPLORERS HALL (► 31)
UNION STATION (► 46)

THE SMITHSONIAN MUSEUMS

These museums entertain and educate millions of children every year on everything from aardvarks and airplanes to singing insects and space suits. Of special interest are the dinosaurs and the insect zoo at the National Museum of Natural History; the Hands-on-History and Hands-on-Science rooms at the National Museum of American History (► 36); "Amazonia" and the Invertebrate House at the National Zoological Park (► 55); the IMAX films at the National Air and Space Museum (► 43); and the Discovery Theater with its puppet shows, plays, and storytelling.

National Museum of Natural History G5 Constitution Avenue and 10th Street NW 202/357-2700 Daily 10–5.30 Smithsonian, Federal Triangle Free

National Museum of American History G5 Constitution Avenue and 14th Street NW 202/357-2700 Daily 10–5.30 Smithsonian, Federal Triangle Free

National Zoological Park E1–F1 3001 Connecticut Avenue NW 202/673-4717 Daily 6–6.15PM Woodley Park-Zoo Free

National Air and Space Museum H5 Independence Avenue at 6th Street SW 202/357-2700 Daily 10–5.30 L'Enfant Plaza Free

Discovery Theater G5 900 Jefferson Drive SW 200/357-1500 Plays Mon–Fri: 10AM, 11.30AM Smithsonian Inexpensive

CAPITAL CHILDREN'S MUSEUM

Everything here is as messy as if a horde of happy children had played with everything for years—and they have. Permanent exhibitions explore Mexican and Japanese cultures, animation, still-life drawing, and children's art.

J4 800 3rd Street NE 202/675-4120 Daily 10–5 6 Union Station Inexpensive

HARD ROCK CAFÉ

Kids and their parents love the up-beat rock and roll hall of fame atmosphere and good-sized portions at this restaurant, complete with its own line of T-shirts and baseball caps.

G4 999 E Street NW 202/737-7625 Mon–Fri 11AM–midnight; Sat, Sun 11AM–1AM Metro Center

NATIONAL AQUARIUM

Opened in 1873, the aquarium has a touch tank, sea

turtles, eels, tropical and freshwater fish, and shark and piranha feeding at 2PM on alternate days.
G5 14th Street and Pennsylvania Avenue NW 202/482-2825 Daily 9–5 Federal Triangle Inexpensive

NATIONAL ZOOLOGICAL PARK

Within the 5ha (160 acres) landscaped by Frederick Law Olmsted, Sr., in 1889, zoo designers have constantly renovated enclosures to provide natural settings for birds, hoofed stock, komodo dragons, pygmy hippopotamuses, big cats, monkeys, and much more. The quiet Invertebrate House houses many rarely seen animals.
E1–F1 3001 Connecticut Avenue NW 202/673-4717 Grounds daily 6AM–6.15PM. Animal buildings May to mid-Sep: daily 10–6. Mid-Sep to Apr: daily 10–4.30. "Amazonia" daily 10–4 Snack bars Woodley Park-Zoo Free. Parking charge

NAVY MUSEUM

Big ships, cannons, submarines, and periscopes; kids here can pretend to conquer the seven seas.
K7 9th and M Streets SE, Building 76 202/433-4882 Mon–Fri 9–4; Sat, Sun, hols 10–5 Eastern Market, Navy Yard Free

PLANET HOLLYWOOD

Owned by movie stars and decorated with cinema memorabilia, this restaurant specializes in burgers, pasta, and other American favourites. A merchandizing arm sells everything from caps to jackets.
G5 1101 Pennsylvania Avenue NW 202/783-7827 Daily 11AM–10.30PM Federal Triangle

PUPPET COMPANY PLAYHOUSE

Located in Glen Echo Park, MD, this troupe presents plays beloved by children of all ages.
Off map at A1 7300 MacArthur Boulevard, Glen Echo, MD 301/320-6668 Inexpensive. Free annual puppet exhibition No. 29

FAO SCHWARZ

This shop stocks the best (or at least the most expensive) toys, dolls, children's books, and more.
D3 3222 M Street NW 202/342-2285 Mon–Sat 10–9; Sun 11–6 Café

WASHINGTON DOLL'S HOUSE AND TOY MUSEUM

This museum has an extensive collection of Victorian dolls, doll's houses, toys, and games.
Off map at D1 5236 44th Street NW 202/244-0024 Tue–Sat 10–5; Sun noon–5 Friendship Heights Inexpensive

Tigers and other endangered species are bred at the National Zoological Park

BABY-SITTERS

For sitters, check with your hotel concierge or call:
Mothers' Aides Inc.
Box 7088, Fairfax Station, VA 22039 703/250-0700
WeeSit
10681 Oak Thrust Court, Burke, VA 22015 703/764-1542.

Libraries & Archives

A BOOKWORM'S PARADISE

When listing the reasons to live inside the Capital Beltway, many Washingtonians praise the literary scene. Museums and historic sites have extensive bookshelves, crammed with publications related to museum collections and historic events, and most have libraries open to researchers. Throughout the city, specialized collections are open to anyone with an interest, as well as scholars and students of everything from Jewish-American military history to Shakespeare.

In the Top 25

LIBRARY OF CONGRESS (➤ 48)
NATIONAL ARCHIVES (➤ 41)

BETHUNE MUSEUM AND ARCHIVES

Preserving and documenting African-American women's participation in American history is the mission of this site, in a Victorian house near historic Logan Circle. Mary McLeod Bethune, political activist, educator, and founder of the National Council of Negro Women, once lived here. The house also served as the Council's headquarters.
G3 1318 Vermont Avenue NW 202/332-1233 Sep–May: Mon–Fri 10–4. Jun–Aug: Mon–Sat 10–4 U Street-Cardozo, McPherson Square Free

FOLGER SHAKESPEARE LIBRARY

The world's most comprehensive collection of Shakespeare's works is included in this library of 275,000 books, manuscripts, and paintings from and about the European Renaissance.
J5 201 E Capitol SE 202/544-4600 For researchers Mon–Fri 10–4. Guided tours Mon–Fri 11AM; Sat 11AM, 1PM Free Capitol South

HISTORICAL SOCIETY OF WASHINGTON

Text and image collections relating to DC's social history are housed in the ornate Victorian Heurich Mansion, built by a wealthy brewer.
F3 1307 New Hampshire Avenue NW 202/785-2068 Mon–Sat 10–4 Dupont Circle Inexpensive

MARTIN LUTHER KING MEMORIAL LIBRARY

The large, active main branch of the DC public library system, MLK has an extensive Washingtoniana collection, as well as a Black Studies Division. Mies van der Rohe designed the unadorned steel-and-glass building, which opened in 1972 and is softened by Don Miller's mural celebrating the life of Martin Luther King, Jr.
G4 901 G Street NW 202/727-1111 Mon–Thu 10–9; Fri, Sat 10–5.30; Sun 1–5 Gallery Place

MOORLAND-SPINGARN RESEARCH CENTER

The Center includes extensive archives and secondary material about the African diaspora.
H2 500 Howard Place in Founders Library, Howard University 202/806-7239 Mon–Fri 9–4.45 Shaw-Howard University

NATIONAL GEOGRAPHIC SOCIETY LIBRARY

This little-known library houses 50,000 books on geography, natural history, travel, and topics that have long interested the Society, such as polar exploration. Of course, all the Society's publications, including a complete run of the famous yellow magazine begun in 1888, are available. The reading room has an automated catalogue, good light, and warm wood panelling.

F3 17th and M Streets NW 202/857-7783 By appointment, Mon–Fri 1.30–5 Dupont Circle, Farragut North

SMITHSONIAN INSTITUTION LIBRARIES

Collections include images of airplanes of all periods, worldwide flora and fauna, space, film and television, linguistics, palaeobiology, the history of railroads, women's political life, domestic industry, war, peace, and much else besides. Of special note are the Archives of American Art, the National Anthropological Archives, and the Human Studies Film Archives (➤ 39). Contact the Smithsonian's headquarters at the Castle for opening times of individual libraries.

G5 The Castle, Jefferson Drive at 10th Street SW 202/357-2700 Daily 9–5.30 Smithsonian

SUMNER SCHOOL MUSEUM AND ARCHIVES

Architect Adolph Cluss won a Medal for Progress at the Vienna World's Exposition in 1873 for his innovative use of hallways and closets to shield classrooms from exterior noise. The school stood as a model of black education during segregation. It now houses the archives of the DC Public Schools.

F3 17th and M Streets NW 202/727-3419 Mon–Sat 10–5 Dupont Circle

Exhibits at the National Geographic Society

Gardens & Sculpture

Do not let the Washington summer heat keep you from exploring the city's often inspiring, often whimsical sculptures, many of them in lovely gardens with plenty of shade.

In the Top 25

BARTHOLDI FOUNTAIN AT THE U.S. BOTANIC GARDENS (➤ 44)
COLUMBUS PLAZA AT UNION STATION (➤ 46)
F. D. R. & JEFFERSON MEMORIALS (➤ 34)
LINCOLN MEMORIAL (➤ 28)
NEPTUNE'S COURT AT THE LIBRARY OF CONGRESS (➤ 48)
VIETNAM VETERANS MEMORIAL AND CONSTITUTION GARDENS (➤ 30)
WASHINGTON MONUMENT (➤ 33)

THE AWAKENING

The Awakening, by J. Seward Johnson, was originally part of a temporary exhibition. So many Washingtonians appreciated the bearded aluminum giant rising from the tip of Hains Point that it stayed. The surrounding park has jogging and bike paths, tennis, swimming, and golf.
H9 Hains Point, East Potomac Park 202/485-9880, 202/727-6523 24 hours Waterfront Free

BISHOPS GARDEN

Designed around European ruins and a statue of the Prodigal Son, this is a gem in the 23ha (57 acres) at Washington National Cathedral. Plantings include herbs, boxwood, magnolia trees, and tea roses.
C1–D1 Wisconsin and Massachusetts Avenues NW 202/537-6200 May–Labor Day: Mon–Fri 10–9; Sat, Sun 10–4.30. Labor Day–Apr: daily 10–4.30 Tenley Town; 30 series bus south Free

DUMBARTON BRIDGE

Bronze renditions of shaggy prairie animals make an unusual sculptural group on this bridge, nicknamed the Bison Bridge, which spans a section of Rock Creek Park near Georgetown. Take the footpath under the bridge to see the busts of Native Americans, said to be modeled from a death mask of Sitting Bull.
E3 23rd and Q Streets NW 24 hours Dupont Circle Free

DUMBARTON OAKS

In 1944 the international conference leading to the formation of the United Nations was held at this estate, also known for its fine 4ha (10-acre) formal garden. The orangery, rose garden, wisteria, and

FRIENDSHIP ARCH

Located at Chinatown Metro, this gilded arch symbolizes the energy and vitality of Washington's Asian community.
H4 Chinatown, 7th and G Streets NW 24 hours Gallery Place-Chinatown Free

magnificent old shaded terraces make this a must for anyone interested in gardens, or who just wants to rest for just a few moments surrounded by blazing nature.
D2 31st and R Streets NW 202/339-6400 Daily 2–5 Dupont Circle, then bus No. D2 Inexpensive

EINSTEIN MEMORIAL
In the grounds of Washington's National Academy of Sciences, Robert Berks's sculpture depicts the physicist Albert Einstein gently feeding birds and speaking to children.
E5 22nd Street NW and Constitution Avenue, in the grounds of the National Academy of Sciences 24 hours Foggy Bottom Free

GRANT MEMORIAL
General Ulysses S. Grant looks weary from his struggles as he sits on horseback at the foot of Capitol Hill, at the centre of the city's most effective sculptural group of men on horses.
H5 1st Street NW at the foot of Capitol Hill 24 hours Capitol South Free

HIRSHHORN SCULPTURE GARDEN
In this walled, sunken garden, you are surrounded by works by Henry Moore, Max Ernst, Pablo Picasso, Man Ray, and other luminaries.
H5 7th Street and Jefferson Drive SW 202/357-2700 7.30AM–dusk L'Enfant Plaza Free

NATIONAL ARBORETUM
The Arboretum's 180ha (446 acres) invite driving, biking, and hiking. The National Herb Garden and National Bonsai Collection are fascinating, and the Azalea Walk is beautiful in the spring.
M3–N3 3501 New York Avenue NE 202/245-2726 Daily 8–5 Brookland-CUA, then bus No. H6 B2 Free

NATIONAL GALLERY OF ART SCULPTURE GARDEN
Works by Louise Bourgeois, Mark di Suveroi, Roy Lichtenstein, and many other 20th-century artists can be enjoyed in this 2.6ha (6.5-acre garden. The reflecting pool becomes a skating rink in winter.
H5 Between Constitution Avenue and the National Mall, 7th and 9th Street NW 202/737-4215 Mon–Sat 10–5; Sun 11–6. Skating rink winter: daily 11AM–10PM Archives Free. Skating inexpensive

ROCK CREEK PARK
Washingtonians enjoy Rock Creek Park's 729ha (1,800 acres) for picnicking, biking, hiking, tennis, golf, riding, jogging, and the Nature Center and Planetarium.
E1–E3 Nature Center, 5000 Glover Road NW 202/426-6829 Nature Center Wed–Sun 9–5. Grounds daylight hours Woodley Park-Zoo Free

Grant Memorial below Capitol Hill

KOREAN WAR VETERANS MEMORIAL

Dedicated in 1995, this memorial includes 19 life-size figures marching up an incline toward the American flag, a still pool memorializing those who lost their lives in the war, and photographs of the Korean conflict etched into an 18m (60-ft) wall. A memorial of faces, it is a compelling counterpoint to the Vietnam Veterans Memorial wall of names.
E5 Between the Lincoln Memorial and Independence Avenue 202/208-3561 24 hours Free

Places of Worship

THE DC JEWISH COMMUNITY CENTER

First opened in 1926 and completely redesigned in 1990, the Center at 1529 16th Street NW includes a lap pool, gym with steam rooms, auditorium, classrooms, racket courts, library, social hall, gallery, 250-seat theatre, and kosher restaurant. In essence, almost everything a traveller might need to keep fit in mind and body.

Minaret of the Islamic Mosque and Cultural Center

In the Top 25

SHRINE OF THE IMMACULATE CONCEPTION (➤ 49)

US HOLOCAUST MEMORIAL MUSEUM (➤ 35)

ADAS ISRAEL CONGREGATION

Conservative. Highlights of this post-World War II concrete building include a two-story window depicting the Star of David, a 3m (10-ft) bronze menorah by Milton Hebald, and several sculptures by Phillip Rapner depicting Jewish traditions.
Off map at E1 | 2850 Quebec Street NW | 202/362-4433 | Cleveland Park

BET MISH PACHAH SYNAGOGUE

Gay and lesbian congregation.
F3 | 16th & Q Streets NW | 202/833-1638 | Services held at DC Jewish Community Center | Dupont Circle

THE IMANI TEMPLE

African-American Catholic congregation founded by Reverend G. Augustus Stalings, Jr., in 1987.
K5 | 609–11 Maryland Avenue NE | 202/388-8155 | Daily 9–6 | Union Station

ISLAMIC MOSQUE AND CULTURAL CENTER

Calls to the faithful emanate from a 49m (162-ft) minaret. Inside are Persian carpets, ebony and ivory carvings, stained glass, and mosaics.
E2 | 2551 Massachusetts Avenue NW | 202/332-8343 | Cultural Center daily 10.30–4.30. Prayer dawn 10.30PM | Dupont Circle

METROPOLITAN AFRICAN METHODIST EPISCOPAL CHURCH

This red-brick Gothic-revival church, known as the national cathedral of the AME movement, was completed in 1886, paid for by former slaves, and built by African-American artisans.
G3 | 1518 M Street NW | 202/331-1426 | Mon–Sat 10–6 | Home-cooked lunch Thu, Fri 11–2 | Farragut North

MOUNT ZION HERITAGE CENTER AND METHODIST CHURCH

Established in 1816, this congregation educated black children and adults, created DC's first black library, and served as a stop on the underground railroad that transported Southern slaves to the free North. The church is known for its elaborate pressed-tin ceiling, engravings by African artisans, and embellished cast-iron pillars.
E3 | 1334 29th Street NW | 202/234-0148 | Easily arranged by appointment | Dupont Circle

ST. JOHN'S EPISCOPAL CHURCH

Presidents have worshipped in Pew 54 since the church was built by Benjamin Latrobe in a Greek Cross form in 1816. Later additions include a Doric portico and cupola.

F4 1525 H Street NW 202/347-8766 Mon–Fri 8–4; Sat 9–3; Sun services 8, 9, 11 McPherson Square

ST. MARY'S EPISCOPAL CHURCH

James Renwick designed this redbrick 1887 Gothic-revival church for DC's first black Protestant Episcopal congregation. The building has a timber roof and French painted-glass windows depicting St. Cyprian and other African religious leaders. A garden provides peace and quiet downtown.

E4 728 23rd Street NW 202/333-3985 Daily 9–4 Foggy Bottom

ST. MATTHEW'S CATHEDRAL

President John F. Kennedy's funeral mass was held in this plain Renaissance-style church, the seat of Washington's Catholic archbishop. Inside there are stunning mosaics and gilded Corinthian capitals.

F3 1725 Rhode Island Avenue NW 202/347-3215 Sun–Fri 7–6.30; Sat 8–7 Farragut North

TEMPLE MICAH

This intimate postmodern masonry building has great acoustics and a friendly Reform congregation.

D1 2829 Wisconsin Avenue 202/333-4808 Foggy Bottom

WASHINGTON HEBREW CONGREGATION

Reform congregation.

Off map at C1 3935 Macomb Street NW 202/362-7100 Cleveland Park

WASHINGTON NATIONAL CATHEDRAL

On 30 September 1990, President George Bush and thousands of other guests watched the placement of the final stone of this Gothic-style building, complete with flying buttresses, 158m (518-ft) nave, rose window made up of 10,500 pieces of stained glass, stone barrel vaults, and fanciful gargoyles. The stone carving in this, the world's sixth-largest cathedral, is extraordinary. Author Helen Keller is buried within.

C1–D1 Wisconsin and Massachusetts Avenues NW 202/537-6200 May–Labor Day: Mon–Fri 10–9; Sat, Sun 10–4.30. Labor Day–Apr: daily 10–4.30 Tenley Town, then 30 series bus south

QUIET PLACES

Do not overlook the Hall of Remembrance in the US Holocaust Memorial Museum. This space invites quiet, nondenomi-national contemplation, as does Barnett Newman's *14 Stations of the Cross* hanging on the concourse level of the National Gallery of Art.

Washington National Cathedral

Views

In the Top 25

CEDAR HILL (➤ 50)
CUSTIS-LEE MANSION AT ARLINGTON NATIONAL CEMETERY (➤ 26)
JOHN F. KENNEDY CENTER ROOF TERRACE (➤ 27)
LIBRARY OF CONGRESS CAFETERIA (➤ 48)
US CAPITOL, WEST FACE (➤ 45)
WASHINGTON MONUMENT (➤ 33)

HOTEL WASHINGTON ROOF TERRACE

This landmark is the oldest continuously operating hotel in the city, known since its opening in 1918 as "the hotel with the view." The terrace overlooks the White House and the Washington Monument, and is *the* place for afternoon tea or sunset cocktails.

G4 515 15th Street NW 202/638-5900 14 Apr–30 Oct: daily 11.30AM–1AM McPherson Square Expensive

OLD POST OFFICE BUILDING TOWER

To get your bearings in the city, the clock tower at the Old Post Office has the best view, and the building houses a food court with everything from ice cream to Indian food.

G5 Pennsylvania Avenue at 12th Street NW 202/606-8691 Easter–Labor Day: daily 8AM–11PM. Labor Day–Mar: daily 10–6 Many cafés and restaurants Federal Triangle Free

FRANCIS SCOTT KEY BRIDGE

The pedestrian-friendly Francis Scott Key Bridge, accessible from M Street in Georgetown, is a great place to see the river or for a view of the Georgetown skyline.

The view from the Old Post Office tower

WASHINGTON where to...

EAT

Traditional American *64*
Steak & Seafood *65*
Contemporary American *66*
French *67*
Italian *68*
Spanish, Latin & Tex-Mex *69*
Pan-Asian *70*
Indian, African & Middle Eastern *71*

SHOP

Shopping Districts, Malls & Department Stores *72–73*
Clothing *74*
Markets & Foodstores *75*
Antiques, Crafts & Gifts *76–77*
Books & Music *78–79*

BE ENTERTAINED

Live Music & Comedy Clubs *80*
Bars & Lounges *81*
Theatres *82*
Concert Venues *83*
The Performing Arts & Movies *84*
Sports *85*

STAY

Luxury Hotels *86*
Mid-Range Hotels *87*
Budget Accommodations *88*

Traditional American

PRICES

Expect to pay for a three-course meal per person, excluding drinks:

$ up to $20
$$ up to $35
$$$ more than $35

All restaurants mentioned here take major credit cards. It is usually advisable to make a reservation.

B. SMITH'S ($$–$$$)

Set in the historic presidential waiting room, this restaurant serves Southern barbecued ribs, fried catfish and the house special, Swamp Thing—mustard-seasoned shrimp and crawfish with collard greens.
J4 Union Station, 50 Massachusetts Avenue NE 202/289-6188 Daily lunch, dinner Union Station

CAPITOL CITY BREWING COMPANY ($–$$)

Beer and burgers are the draws at this local brewpub.
G4 1100 New York Avenue NW (corner of 11th & H Streets) 202/628-2222 Daily lunch, dinner Metro Center
J4 2 Massachusetts Avenue NE 202/842-2337 Daily lunch, dinner Union Station

CLYDE'S ($–$$)

This longtime fixture in Georgetown (and other locations in the area) is a good bet for basic steak, burgers, and fish.
D3 3236 M Street NW 202/333-9180 Daily lunch, dinner; Sat, Sun breakfast Foggy Bottom-GWU then bus No. 32, 34, 35, or 36

GEORGIA BROWN'S ($$)

This elegant restaurant attracts government officials, lobbyists, and journalists. Southern specials are on offer.
G4 950 15th Street NW 202/393-4499 Mon–Fri lunch, dinner; Sun brunch, dinner McPherson Square

MARKET LUNCH ($)

Located in Eastern Market, this counter-service eatery features crab cakes, fried fish, and North Carolina barbecue.
K6 225 7th Street SE 202/547-8444 Tue–Sat breakfast, lunch; Sun lunch Eastern Market

THE MONOCLE ($$–$$$)

This is one of the best restaurants for spotting members of Congress sitting near the fireplaces. American food with a Continental touch.
J5 107 D Street NE 202/546-4488 Mon–Fri lunch, dinner Union Station

OLD EBBITT GRILL ($$)

A block from the White House, this is one of Washington's busiest restaurants; oyster bar, pub food, and family fare.
G4 675 15th Street NW 202/347-4800 Daily breakfast, lunch, and dinner Metro Center

OLD GLORY ($–$$)

The flags of six big barbecue-eating Southern states hang from the ceiling in this updated roadhouse, which serves all variations of barbecued pork, beef, and chicken.
D3 3139 M Street NW 202/337-3406 Daily lunch, dinner; Sun all-you-can-eat country brunch Foggy Bottom-GWU, then bus Nos. 32, 35, or 38B

VIDALIA ($$$)

A classy Southern retreat serving shrimp and grits, greens and Vidalia onion casserole.
F3 1990 M Street NW 202/659-1990 Mon–Fri lunch, dinner; Sat, Sun dinner Dupont Circle

Steak & Seafood

CAUCUS ROOM ($$–$$$)
A clubby steak parlour, where the powerful talk politics over rib-eyes and creamed spinach.
H5 401 9th Street NW 202/393-1300 Mon–Fri lunch; Mon–Sat dinner Archives-Navy Memorial

JOHNNY'S HALF SHELL ($$)
An unpretentious bistro, serving top-notch crab cakes, rockfish, and other Eastern Shore dishes.
F3 2002 P Street NW 202/296-2021 Mon–Sat lunch, dinner Dupont Circle

KINKEAD'S ($$$)
One of DC's best restaurants, Kinkead's is an updated seafood restaurant, with fried Ipswich clams, grilled squid, and pepita-encrusted salmon.
F4 2000 Pennsylvania Avenue NW 202/296-7700 Daily lunch, dinner Foggy Bottom

LEGAL SEAFOOD ($$–$$$)
The Boston-based chain now offers Washingtonians an extensive list of New England seafood dishes. Great children's menu.
F4 2020 K Street NW 202/496-1111 Mon–Fri lunch, dinner; Sat, Sun dinner Farragut West
H4 704 7th Street NW 202/347-0007 Daily lunch, dinner Gallery Place-Chinatown

MORTON'S OF CHICAGO ($$$)
It's not the vinyl-boothed room that draws people here, it's the size and the quality of the steaks. If you're really hungry (or sharing), don't miss the 3-pound porterhouse.
D3 3251 Prospect Street NW 202/342-6258 Daily dinner Foggy Bottom, then bus No. 35

THE PALM ($$$)
The father of steakhouses, with huge portions, fresh lobster, and irreverent service.
F3 1225 19th Street NW 202/293-9091 Mon–Fri lunch, dinner; Sat, Sun dinner Dupont Circle

PESCE ($$)
Come here to choose from a long list of seafood dishes (changed daily).
F3 2016 P Street NW 202/466-FISH Mon–Fri lunch, dinner; Sat, Sun dinner Dupont Circle

PRIME RIB ($$$)
Decorated in black and gold like a 1940s supper club, Prime Rib serves its namesake to the posh meat-and-potatoes set. Jacket and tie required.
F4 2020 K Street NW 202/466-8811 Mon–Fri lunch, dinner; Sat dinner Farragut West

SEA CATCH ($$$)
Hidden in a Georgetown courtyard overlooking the C & O Canal, this formal establishment has an outstanding raw bar, offering entrées such as Shenandoah trout stuffed with crab meat and sweet corn.
D3 1054 31st Street NW 202/337-8855 Mon–Sat lunch, dinner Foggy Bottom, then bus No. 35 or 38B

SEAFOOD SOUTHWEST

For a lively and colourful scene, head to the Southwest Fish Wharf (G6 1100 Maine Avenue SW), a floating seafood market at the Potomac River waterfront. From barges and boats, vendors hawk live blue crabs and a wide variety of fish; shucked shellfish, spiced shrimp, and fried fish are available.

BUDGET MEALS

In downtown Washington there are many places where you can get a salad or a sandwich and a drink for under $10. These counter-service chains cater to the office lunch crowd and often have better-than-expected food. Some of the best include Au Bon Pain, Chipotle, Cosi, Firehook Bakery & Coffeehouse, and High Noon Fresh & Ready. Starbucks coffee shops, which populate downtown street corners, also sell salads and sandwiches, and there are a number of Korean-owned salad bars where you can assemble lunch from a huge selection of fresh ingredients. The lower level of Union Station also houses a terrific food court.

Contemporary American

QUALITY DINING

Long considered a city of stodgy restaurants, in recent years Washington has become a very good food town. Talented young American chefs, with their emphasis on regional farm produce and inventive combinations, have contributed largely to the renaissance. The city also has the good fortune to have a chef who was given a two-star rating by the highly regarded *Guide Michelin:* Gérard Pangaud, of Gérard's Place (see main entry, next page).

701 RESTAURANT ($$–$$$)

This very elegant restaurant, with large windows looking out on Pennsylvania Avenue, offers a vodka and caviar bar, and live jazz every night.

H5 701 Pennsylvania Avenue NW 202/393-0701 Mon–Fri lunch, dinner; Sat, Sun dinner Archives

1789 ($$$)

Housed in a historic town house with a large fireplace, 1789 specializes in innovatively prepared game and seafood.

C3 1226 36th Street NW 202/965-1789 Daily dinner Foggy Bottom, then bus No. 32 or 38B

BREADLINE ($)

One-of-a-kind bakery-café that turns out crusty breads, eclectic sandwiches, and homemade soups. A popular spot for White House staffers.

F4 1751 Pennsylvania Avenue NW 202/822-8900 Mon–Fri breakfast, lunch Farragut West

CASHION'S EAT PLACE ($$)

This Adams-Morgan restaurant serves sophisticated versions of home-style meals. You'll find several seafood choices, as well as roast chicken, steak, and lamb.

F2 1819 Columbia Road NW 202/797-1819 Tue–Sat dinner; Sun brunch, dinner Dupont Circle then bus No. L2

DC COAST ($$–$$$)

In a stunning Beaux Arts setting, enjoy Chinese style smoked lobster with crispy spinach, or grilled Angus rib-eye with green chili macaroni and cheese.

G4 1401 K Street NW 202/216-5988 Mon–Fri lunch, dinner; Sat dinner McPherson Square

EQUINOX ($$$)

Uses regional ingredients for fresh, seasonal dishes, including wild rockfish filet over braised fennel or seared Hudson Valley foie gras.

F4 818 Connecticut Avenue NW 202/331-8118 Mon–Fri lunch; daily dinner Farragut West

NEW HEIGHTS ($$$)

Appetizers include grilled bison hanger steak, with entrées such as roasted stuffed skate wing.

E1 2317 Calvert Street NW 202/234-4110 Mon–Sat dinner Woodley Park-Zoo

NORA ($$$)

America's first certified organic restaurant, serving a pricey menu of free-range meats, boutique produce and local seafood.

E3 2132 Florida Avenue NW 202/462-5143 Mon–Sat dinner Dupont Circle

TABARD INN ($$)

With its parlour-like dining rooms and lovely terrace, the Tabard is a pleasure for its organic vegetables and hormone-free beef.

F3 1739 N Street NW 202/ 833-2668 Daily breakfast, lunch, dinner Dupont Circle

French

BIS ($$–$$$)
Located in the Hotel George, Bis offers an extensive wine list to complement appetizers such as snails with artichoke and rabbit galette, and entrées like mussels and duck confit.
J4 15 E Street NW 202/661-2700 Daily breakfast, lunch, dinner Union Station

BISTRO FRANCAIS ($$)
Fixed-price lunches and dinner specials are a good deal in this classic French bistro. Stays open well into the night.
D3 3128 M Street NW 202/338-3830 Daily lunch, dinner Foggy Bottom, then bus No. 35 or 38B

LA CHAUMIERE ($$–$$$)
Like a rustic French inn, this restaurant serves country fare such as cassoulet and bouillabaisse.
E3 2813 M Street NW 202/338-1784 Mon–Fri lunch, dinner; Sat dinner Foggy Bottom

LA COLLINE ($$)
Seafood—fricassée, grilled, or gratinée—is one measure of this consistently excellent Capitol Hill favourite.
J5 400 N Capitol Street NW 202/737-0400 Mon–Fri breakfast, lunch, dinner; Sat dinner Union Station

LA FOURCHETTE ($$)
A bit of Paris in Adams-Morgan, with tin ceiling, bentwood chairs, quasi-Post-Impressionist murals, and sturdy bistro cuisine such as veal or lamb shanks.
F2 2429 18th Street NW 202/332-3077 Mon–Fri lunch, dinner; Sat–Sun brunch, dinner Woodley Park-Zoo, then bus Nos. 90, 92, 93 or 96

GÉRARD'S PLACE ($$$)
Gérard Pangaud takes French fare to greater heights; try the poached lobster.
G4 915 15th Street NW 202/737-4445 Mon–Fri lunch, dinner; Sat dinner McPherson Square

MARCEL'S ($$$)
Belgian-influenced French cuisine in an elegant setting. Live piano music in the bar; shuttle service to nearby Kennedy Center.
E4 2401 Pennsylvania Avenue NW 202/296-1166 Daily dinner Foggy Bottom-GWU

MICHEL RICHARD CITRONELLE ($$$)
Consistently among Washington's top restaurants for its creative contemporary food.
D3 Latham Hotel, 3000 M Street NW 202/625-2150 Daily breakfast, lunch, dinner Foggy Bottom, then bus No. 35 or 38B

MONTMARTE ($$)
A French bistro with an open kitchen and friendly environment. Braised rabbit leg over pasta is a favourite.
K6 327 7th Street SE 202/544-1244 Tue–Sun lunch, dinner Eastern Market

AFTERNOON TEA

For a relaxing respite after a day of touring, nothing beats afternoon tea served in an elegant and serene setting. Several of Washington's hotels offer tea service, including: **Four Seasons** (2800 Pennsylvania Avenue NW 202/342-0444 Mon–Fri 3–5; Sat, Sun 4–5.30); **Henley Park** (926 Massachusetts Avenue NW 202/638-5200 Daily 4–6); **Jefferson** (1200 16th Street NW 202/347-2200 Daily 3–5); and the **Renaissance Mayflower** (1127 Connecticut Avenue 202/347-3000 Mon–Sat 3-5; Sun 3.30–5.30).
There are also two Asian-inspired tearooms that are definitely worth a stop: **Ching Ching Cha** (1063 Wisconsin Avenue NW Tue–Sun); and **Teaism** (800 Connecticut Avenue NW 202/835-2233 Mon–Fri, 2.30–5.30; 400 Eighth Street NW 202/638-6010 Daily 2.30–5.30).

Italian

DOOR-TO-DOOR DINING

If you find yourself hungry in your hotel room, but don't want room-service food, try one of several pizza delivery services. Domino's is the largest chain, with many locations. Pizza Hut has a few delivery outlets. **Armand's** ☎ 202/547-6600 on Capitol Hill or 202/363- 5500 for upper Wisconsin Avenue; **Geppetto** ☎ 202/ 333-4315, in Georgetown; and **Trio Pizza** ☎ 202/232-5611, near Dupont Circle. All deliver.

CAFÉ MILANO ($$$)
Risottos and grilled fish are worth trying in this favourite Georgetown gathering place.
E3 ✉ 3251 Prospect Street NW ☎ 202/333-6183 Daily lunch, dinner Foggy Bottom, then bus No. 36 or 38B

GALILEO ($$$)
Twice daily Galileo changes its menu using homemade items from bread-sticks to mozzarella, and Italian specialties of grilled fish, game birds, and veal. Extensive wine list.
F4 ✉ 1110 21st Street NW ☎ 202/293-7191 Mon–Fri lunch, dinner; Sat, Sun dinner Foggy Bottom

I. RICCHI ($$$)
This airy Tuscan dining room, with terracotta tiles and floral frescoes, serves spit-roasted meats and a seasonal menu. It attracts the business crowd.
F3 ✉ 1220 19th Street NW ☎ 202/835-0459 Mon–Fri lunch, dinner; Sat dinner Dupont Circle

LUIGINO ($$)
This dependable trattoria turns out traditional and modern dishes in a former art deco bus station.
G4 ✉ 1100 New York Avenue NW (corner of 12th and H Streets) ☎ 202/371-0595 Mon–Fri lunch, daily dinner Metro Center

OBELISK ($$$)
American chef Peter Pastan presents creative, authentic Italian cuisine; fixed price five-course menu.
F3 ✉ 2029 P Street NW ☎ 202/872-1180 Tue–Sat dinner Dupont Circle

PASTA MIA ($)
Choose from among 30 pasta dishes at this better-than-average neighbourhood restaurant.
F2 ✉ 1790 Columbia Road NW ☎ 202/328-9114 Mon–Sat dinner Woodley Park-Zoo, then bus No. 90, 92, 93, 96, or 98

PIZZERIA PARADISO ($)
This pizzeria, with a trompe l'œil ceiling, serves deliciously fresh pizzas, salads, and sandwiches.
F3 ✉ 2029 P Street NW ☎ 202/223-1245 Daily lunch, dinner Dupont Circle

PRIMI PIATTI ($$$)
House specials include pastas, antipasti, and grilled items made with quality ingredients.
F4 ✉ 2013 1 Street NW ☎ 202/223-3600 Mon–Fri lunch, dinner; Sat dinner Farragut West

TEATRO GOLDONI ($$–$$$)
Theatrical decor sets the stage for chef Fabrizio Aielli's Venetian cuisine. Ask for the *fritto misto di mare* (fried seafood) appetizer. Vegetarian entrées available regularly.
F4 ✉ 1909 K Street NW ☎ 202/955-9494 Mon–Fri lunch, dinner; Sat dinner Farragut West or Farragut North

LA TOMATE ($$$)
Enjoy homemade pastas, fresh fish, and other simple dishes at this busy trattoria.
F3 ✉ 1701 Connecticut Avenue NW ☎ 202/667-5505 Daily lunch, dinner Dupont Circle

Spanish, Latin & Tex-Mex

ANDALE ($$)
Start with a margarita, move on to seared sea bass, and end with churros (Mexican doughnuts) dipped in hot chocolate.
H5 407 7th Street NW 202/783-3133 Mon–Sat lunch, dinner Archives-Navy Memorial

BANANA CAFÉ & PIANO BAR ($)
Stick with the Cuban and Puerto Rican dishes at this lively, colourful eatery that features Latino artwork and entertainment each night.
K6 500 Eighth Street SE 202/543-5906 Mon–Sat lunch, dinner; Sun brunch, dinner Eastern Market

CAFÉ ATLANTICO ($$–$$$)
Adventurous Latin American cuisine, featuring jerk quail and duck confit tacos.
H5 405 8th Street NW 202/393-0812 Mon–Sat lunch, dinner; Sun dinner Archives-Navy Memorial

GABRIEL ($$)
Latin-inspired menu with a twist; whole roast suckling pig at Sunday champagne brunch.
F3 2121 P Street NW (in the Radisson Barcelo Hotel) 202/956-6690 Daily breakfast; Sunday brunch; Tue–Sat dinner; Wed–Fri happy hour with tapas Dupont Circle

THE GRILL FROM IPANEMA ($$)
The Brazilian menu at this Adams-Morgan restaurant ranges from spicy seafood stews to traditional *feijoada*.
F2 1858 Columbia Road NW 202/986-0757 Mon–Fri dinner; Sat, Sun lunch, dinner Woodley Park-Zoo, then walk nine blocks or bus No. 90, 99, or L2

JALEO ($–$$)
Choose from dozens of hot and cold tapas at this lively gathering place.
H5 480 7th Street NW 202/628-7949 Daily lunch, dinner Archives-Navy Memorial

LAURIOL PLAZA ($$)
Simple, Spanish/South American restaurant, whose specials include mesquite wood- and charcoal-grilled meats and vegetables, and freshly made tortillas and nachos.
F2 1835 18th Street NW 202/387-0035 Daily lunch, dinner Dupont Circle

RED SAGE ($$$)
In this faux-adobe warren of dining rooms, peppers are in everything except desserts. Portions and prices are big. There is a chili bar and café upstairs.
G4 605 14th Street NW 202/638-4444 Mon–Fri lunch, dinner; Sat,Sun dinner. Chili bar: Mon–Sat lunch, dinner; Sun dinner Metro Center

TABERNA DEL ALABARDERO ($$$)
Attentive service and plush decor create a romantic setting for traditional Spanish cuisine. Extensive wine list.
F4 1776 I Street NW (entrance on 18th Street) 202/429-2200 Mon–Fri lunch, dinner; Sat dinner Farragut West

BETHESDA FEASTING

Bethesda, a short distance from the District line in Maryland, has in the past few years become a veritable city of restaurants. Within a few blocks of the Bethesda Metro station there are more than 200 eateries, providing many different international dining options:
Cesco Trattoria (Italian 4871 Cordell Avenue 301/654-8333); **Faryab Afghan Cuisine** (Afghan 4917 Cordell Avenue 301/951-3484); **Grapeseed American Bistro and Wine Bar** (Modern American 4865 C. Cordell Avenue 301/986-9592); **Green Papaya** (Vietnamese 4922 Elm Street 301/654-8986); **Jaleo** (Latin American 7271 Woodmont Avenue 301/913-0003); **La Miche** (French 7905 Norfolk Avenue 301/986-0707); **Matuba** (Japanese 4918 Cordell Avenue 301/652-7449): and **Tara Thai** (Thai 4828 Bethesda Avenue 301/657-0488).
If your touring feet are tired, the Bethesda 8 trolley stops at the Metro station and runs through the restaurant area. It operates Mon–Thu 7AM–midnight; Fri 7AM–2AM; Sat 6PM–2AM.

Pan-Asian

CHINATOWN

After years of decline, Washington's Chinatown is in the midst of a revitalization. With the arrival of the MCI Center, a popular sports arena, chain restaurants have been popping up near the H Street corridor. But many of the old Chinese standbys remain: **Eat First** (see main entry this page); **Full Kee** ✉ 509 H Street NW; **Hunan Chinatown** ✉ 624 H Street NW; **Mr. Yung's** ✉ 740 6th Street NW; and **Tony Cheng's Seafood Restaurant and Mongolian Restaurant** ✉ 619 H Street NW. Burma (see main entry this page) is also located in this area.

BURMA ($)

A Chinatown alternative to Chinese food. The Burmese specialties include mango pork and tamarind fish. Start your meal with batter-dipped fried eggplant or squash, with spicy dips.
H4 ✉ 740 6th Street NW ☎ 202/638-1280 Mon–Fri lunch, dinner; Sat, Sun dinner Gallery Place-Chinatown

BUSARA ($$)

This Thai restaurant, stylish in black rubber, brushed steel, and lacquer, stands out for its unusual red curry duck and cellophane noodles with three kinds of mushroom.
C2 ✉ 2340 Wisconsin Avenue NW ☎ 202/337-2340 Daily lunch, dinner Foggy Bottom, then bus No. 34 or 36

EAT FIRST ($)

An unassuming restaurant that is one of Chinatown's best; terrific shrimp dishes.
H4 ✉ 609 H Street NW ☎ 202/289-1703 Daily lunch, dinner Gallery Place-Chinatown

MALAYSIA KOPITIAM ($–$$)

An exotic trip to Malaysia, complete with a photo album picturing each dish on the menu.
F3 ✉ 1827 M Street ☎ 202/833-6232 Daily lunch, dinner Farragut North or Dupont Circle

OODLES NOODLES ($)

Satisfying meal-in-a-bowl soups from various Asian countries
F3 ✉ 1120 19th Street NW ☎ 202/293-3138 Mon–Sat lunch, dinner; Sun dinner Farragut North

QUEEN BEE ($)

One of many Vietnamese restaurants in this Arlington neighbourhood; top-notch spring rolls and grilled dishes.
A5 ✉ 3181 Wilson Boulevard ☎ 703/527-3444 Daily lunch, dinner Clarendon

SAIGON GOURMET ($$)

Popular Vietnamese dining room; try the grilled pork with rice crêpes.
E1 ✉ 2635 Connecticut Avenue NW ☎ 202/265-1360 Daily lunch, dinner Woodley Park-Zoo

STAR OF SIAM ($)

Thai food with an authentic kick; interesting noodle and curry dishes.
F3 ✉ 1136 19th Street NW ☎ 202/785-2839 Mon–Sat lunch, dinner; Sun dinner Farragut North

SUSHI-KO ($$)

Washington's longest-running sushi bar, a modern space serving raw seafood, cooked specials and French wines.
C2 ✉ 2309 Wisconsin Avenue ☎ 202/333-4187 Tue–Fri lunch, dinner; Sat–Mon dinner Foggy Bottom-GWU, then bus No. 30, 32, 34, 35, or 36

TEN PENH ($$–$$$)

A hip scene with Asian fusion cuisine, including dishes such as grilled wasabi mashed potatoes or sesame and cilantro crusted salmon with Philippine Shanghai-style fried rice.
G5 ✉ 1001 Pennsylvania Avenue NW ☎ 202/393-4500 Mon–Fri lunch, dinner; Sat dinner Federal Triangle

Indian, African & Middle Eastern

AATISH ON THE HILL ($–$$)
Choose from a variety of tandoori, biryani, and other Pakistani dishes, or try the house special, shahi korma, chunks of lamb in a sauce of yogurt and spices.
K6 609 Pennsylvania Avenue SE 202/544-0931 Mon–Sat lunch, dinner; Sun dinner Eastern Market

BACCHUS ($$)
An intimate Lebanese restaurant in a basement; put together a meal from the long list of appetizers.
F3 1827 Jefferson Place NW 202/785-0734 Mon–Fri lunch, dinner; Sat dinner Dupont Circle

THE BOMBAY CLUB ($$–$$$)
A block from the White House, this beautiful Indian restaurant emulates a private British club in 19th-century India. The breads are excellent, and the seafood dishes, such as lobster Malabar, are superb.
F4 815 Connecticut Avenue NW 202/659-3727 Mon–Fri lunch, dinner; Sat dinner; Sun brunch, dinner Farragut West

BUKOM CAFÉ ($)
Sunny African pop music, and a spicy West African menu filled with goat, lamb, chicken, and vegetable entrées brighten this two-story dining room decked out with potted palms and kente cloth. Open late and live music nightly.
F2 2442 18th Street NW 202/265-4600 Daily dinner Woodley Park-Zoo, then bus No. 92 or 96

HERITAGE INDIA ($$)
A consistently excellent Indian restaurant. House specials include lamb vindaloo, tandoori jumbo prawns and stuffed bell pepper.
C2 2400 Wisconsin Avenue 202/333-3120 Sun–Fri lunch, dinner; Sat dinner Foggy Bottom-GWU, then bus No. 30, 32, 34, 35 or 36

LEBANESE TAVERNA ($–$$)
A good all-around Lebanese restaurant, with dependable food and pleasant surroundings. For a great group activity, order a meze (selection of appetizers).
E1 2641 Connecticut Avenue NW 202/265-8681 Mon–Sat lunch, dinner; Sun dinner Woodley Park-Zoo

MARRAKESH ($$)
In this Moroccan restaurant, on a block of auto repair and supply shops, you share a fixed-price feast with everyone at your table and eat without cutlery. Belly dancers put on nightly shows.
H4 617 New York Avenue NW 202/393-9393 Daily dinner Gallery Place-Chinatown

MESKEREM ($)
Ask for the upstairs dining room in this Ethiopian restaurant, where you can sit on cushions, eat from wicker-basket tables, and scoop up spicy stews and vegetables with spongy injera bread.
F2 2434 18th Street NW 202/462-4100 Daily lunch, dinner Woodley Park-Zoo, then bus No. 90, 92, 93, 96 or 98

ADAMS-MORGAN EATING

Adams-Morgan, the city's most multi-cultural neighbourhood, is crowded, bustling, and filled with ethnic restaurants. A walk along 18th Street leads past: **Bukom Café** (West African, see main entry this page); **The Diner** (all-night diner 2453 18th Street); **Fasika's** (Ethiopian 2447 18th Street); **Little Fountain Café** (international 2339 18th Street); **Meskerem** (Ethiopian, see main entry this page); **San Marco** (Italian 2305 18th Street); and **Saigonnais** (Vietnamese 2307 18th Street).

Shopping Districts, Malls & Department Stores

OPENING HOURS

Stores open Monday to Saturday 10 to 7 (or 8). Some have extended hours on Thursday while those in shopping or tourist areas are often open on Sunday from 10 or noon until 5 or 6.

ADAMS-MORGAN

Bohemian, eccentric, multicultural Adams-Morgan, within three blocks of 18th Street NW and Columbia Road, has some truly unusual shopping. Look for Afro-centric apparel and accessories, Haitian art, hand-crafted jewellery, 1950s relics, and Skynear and Company, the most fashionable eclectic home decorating shop in the city.

✉ Skynear: 2122 18th Street NW ☎ 202/797-7160

CHEVY CHASE PAVILION

The Pavilion, a conservatory-style building near the Mazza Gallerie, houses such stores as Country Road Australia, Joan Van, and Gazelle Wearable Art, among others. The mall's Canyon Café, Cheesecake Factory, California Pizza Kitchen, and Mozzarella's compete with the usual mall food court.

Off map at C1 ✉ 5335 Wisconsin Avenue NW ☎ 202/686-5335 Mon–Fri 10–8; Sat 10–6; Sun 12–5 Friendship Heights

CITY PLACE MALL

For discounted brands look at Nordstrom Rack, Ross, Marshall's, Shoe Rack, Nine West, and dozens of other retailers. Relax afterwards at the movies (10 screens) or grab a bite at the food court.

Off map at H1 ✉ 8661 Colesville Road, Silver Spring MD ☎ 301/589-1091 Mon–Sat 10–9; Sun 12–6 Silver Spring

CONNECTICUT AVENUE

North of Dupont Circle, Connecticut Avenue provides a lively mix of restaurants and stores. Look for modern furniture, housewares, shoes, coffee bars, and bookstores. South of the Circle, Connecticut is home to classy department stores and boutiques, especially for women.

E1–F4

EASTERN MARKET

Gentrified Capitol Hill retains the Eastern Market, where you'll find vendors of seasonal produce outdoors on weekends and purveyors of fresh meats, fish, cheeses, baked goods, and prepared foods (especially Mexican and Italian) six days a week. Crafts on Saturday, flea market Sunday, with an additional flea market across the street both weekend days. Surrounding the market are antiques stores and secondhand clothing stores. Coffee bars sell restorative drinks. For breakfast or lunch, don't overlook the venerable Market Lunch, which serves old-style ham and eggs, enormous flapjacks with rich blueberry topping, and the city's best crab cakes.

K6 ✉ Pennsylvania Avenue and 7th Street SE Tue–Sat 7–6; Sun 9–4 Eastern Market

FASHION CENTER

Macy's and Nordstrom anchor the 160 shops in this Pentagon City mall.

Nordstrom's clerks are superbly trained to assist you, whether you are browsing or buying a fur coat. Across the street you'll find Borders Books and Music and several discount housewares and clothing outlets.
D8 1100 S Hayes Street at Army-Navy Drive and I-395 S 703/415-2400 Mon–Sat 10–9.30; Sun 11–6 Pentagon City

GEORGETOWN PARK

The spacious, three-level mall is a delight for anyone heading to Wisconsin and M, the heart of George-town shopping. Many galleries, antiques stores, and boutiques are within an easy walk. The crowd is young and hip; apparel and decorator shops are as tasteful as they are pricey.
D3 3222 M Street NW 202/298-5577 Mon–Sat 10–9; Sun 12–6 Foggy Bottom, then bus No. 35 or 38B

HECHT AND COMPANY

Hecht's, the major local department store, is well laid out and diverse, so you can find everything from the conservaiive to the trendy.
G4 12th and G Streets NW 202/628-6661 Daily 10–8 Metro Center

MAZZA GALLERIE

This fancy mall offers ritzy Neiman Marcus; the discount Filene's Basement (with 40 other shops offering cookware including Williams-Sonoma and Laura Ashley Home); good women's shoes (Stephane Kélian); maternity wear for the fashion conscious (Pea in the Pod); and one-of-a-kind furnishings and gifts with a southwestern flavour (Skynear and Company).
Off map at C1 5300 Wisconsin Avenue NW 202/966-6114 Mon–Fri 10–8; Sat 10–6; Sun 12–5 Friendship Heights

POTOMAC MILLS MALL

This big deal of outlet malls is now Virginia's largest tourist attraction, with retailers such as Ikea, J. C. Penney, and Marshall's, 15 movie theatres, and a food court offering everything from ice cream to sushi.
Off map at B10 3900 Potomac Mills Circle, Prince William, VA (48km (30mi) south of DC off I-95) 703/643-1770 Daily 11–8

SHOPS AT NATIONAL PLACE

Useful to know about because it's well located in the National Press Club. Keep your eyes peeled for celebrities as you shop in Sharper Image, Banana Republic, and Victoria's Secret.
G4 F Street NW between 13th and 14th 202/662-1250 Metro Center

UNION STATION

The city's main railway station also doubles as one of the US's most pleasant shopping malls where you can wander along marble-floored avenues under vaulted ceilings. Good for gifts.
J4 50 Massachusetts Avenue, NE 202/371-9441 Mon–Sat 10–9; Sun noon–6 Union Station

STAY COOL

Washington summers are only bearable because of air conditioning, and the malls crank up the coolers to accommodate shoppers, diners, and movie-goers. So when the heat gets to you, it may be time to "shop til you drop."

Clothing

UNDERSTATED ELEGANCE

Washingtonians cultivate a studied casualness, but high-fashion shopping is plentiful in addition to the classy stores in the Watergate and Willard hotels. If you want office or tourist attire, you can get great buys almost everywhere.

BRITCHES OF GEORGETOWN

Stylish men come to these two stores for smart traditional clothing.
F4 1776 K Street NW 202/347-8994 Mon–Fri 10–7; Sat 10–6 Farragut North or West
D3 1247 Wisconsin Avenue NW 202/338-3330 Mon–Fri 10–7; Sat 10–6; Sun 12–6 Foggy Bottom, then bus No. 35 or 38B

BROOKS BROTHERS

A real institution (founded 1818), the US's oldest men's store.
F4 1201 Connecticut Avenue 202/659-4650 Mon–Fri 9.30–7; Sat 9.30–6; Sun 12–5 Farragut North

BURBERRYS

The store that introduced Americans to the trenchcoat also sells other fine traditional, garments.
F3 1155 Connecticut Avenue NW 202/463-3000 Mon–Fri 9.30–7; Sat 9.30–6; Sun 12–5 Dupont Circle, Farragut North

CHANEL

Chanel's third-largest store in America is in the Willard Hotel, full of pricey, desirable women's clothes and accessories.
G4 1455 Pennsylvania Avenue NW 202/638-5055 Mon–Sat 10–6 Metro Center

FORECAST

Well-known for their excellent service and for their stylish, classic clothing for women.
K6 218 7th Street SE 202/547-7337 Tue–Fri 11–7; Sat 10–6; Sun 12–5 Eastern Market

HECHT'S

Downtown's only remaining department store. Contemporary brands for men, women, and children.
G4 12th & G Streets NW 202/628-6661 Mon–Sat 10–8; Sun 12–6 Metro Center

J. PRESS

The Ivy League look since 1902.
F4 1801 L Street NW 202/857-0120 Mon–Sat 9.30–6 Farragut West

KHISMET WEARABLE ART

Unusual and beautiful designs for men and women in African fabrics.
F2 1800 Belmont Road NW 202/234-7778 Sat 1–8; Sun 1–6, or by appointment Dupont Circle

KOBOS

West African clothing, accessories, and African music.
F2 2444 18th Street NW 202/332-9580 Mon–Sat 11–8 Dupont Circle

RIZIK BROTHERS

A locally famous ladies' outfitters, known for designer clothing and expert service.
F3 1100 Connecticut Avenue NW 202/223-4050 Mon–Sat 9–6; Thu until 8 Farragut North

TOAST & STRAWBERRIES

Original clothing from around the world, plus art work and art wear.
F3 1608 20th Street NW 202/234-1212 Mon–Sat 11–7; Sun 1–6 Dupont Circle

Markets & Foodstores

DEAN & DELUCA
Occupying one of the 19th-century farmers' markets on Georgetown's main street, this New York export offers thousands of lovely products, from bakery goods and cheese, to designer vegetables, salads, and elegant entrées, coffee, and pastries.
D3 3276 M Street NW 202/342-2500 Sun–Thu 10–8; Fri, Sat 10–9 Foggy Bottom, then bus No. 38B

EASTERN MARKET
The source of the freshest produce in Washington (➤ 72).
K6 7th and C Streets SE 202/546-2698 Tue–Sat 7–6; Sun 9–4 Eastern Market

THE FRENCH MARKET
This market continues to educate the local palate with home-made pâtés, escargots, baguettes, croissants, and French cheeses.
D2 1626–32 Wisconsin Avenue NW 202/338-4828 Tue–Sat 8.30–6 Tenley Town

FRESH FIELDS WHOLE FOODS MARKET
Look to this outlet of the small national chain for wonderful, mostly organic foods and old-fashioned customer service. There's delicious bread, and a gourmet delicatessen, while the oatmeal cookies with maple sugar icing can't be beaten.
Off map at C1 4530 40th Street NW 202/237-5800 Mon–Sat 8AM–10PM; Sun 8–8 Tenleytown

A LITTERI
Situated in the heart of the wholesale food market since 1932, this Italian old-timer is worth the short cab ride from downtown. You'll find more than 100 olive oils and wines to go with every pasta dish you can dream up.
K3 517 Morse Street NE 202/544-0183 Tue, Wed 8–4; Thu, Fri 8–5; Sat 8–3 Union Station, then bus No. D8 or take a cab

LAWSON'S
Single professionals come here for salads, prepared entrées, wines, and baked goodies.
F3 1350 Connecticut Avenue NW 202/775-0400 Mon–Fri 7.30AM–8PM; Sat 10–6 Dupont Circle

RED SAGE GENERAL STORE
An outgrowth of the popular southwestern restaurant next door, this store sells chili peppers and hot-hot-hot to mild salsa, fancy olive oils, herbal vinegars, fresh-baked breads, and desserts.
G4 14th and F Streets NW 202/638-3276 Mon–Fri 8–3 Metro Center

UPTOWN BAKERS
A favourite among many Washingtonians for its wonderful bakery products; you can also buy take-away soups and sandwiches here.
Off map at E1 3313 Connecticut Avenue NW 202/ 362-6262 Mon–Sat 7AM–7.30PM; Sun 7.30–7 Cleveland Park

SHOPPING IN STYLE

Washington is a city for gourmets and it's hard to resist the high-quality foods on offer in specialist shops. The atmosphere in the markets makes shopping fun, especially when prices are often lower than in supermarkets.

Antiques, Crafts & Gifts

TREASURE-HUNTING

Georgetown, Adams-Morgan, Dupont Circle, and the 7th Street art corridor are abundantly supplied with galleries, boutiques, and specialist stores.

MUSEUM SHOPS

No serious shopper should overlook them. In addition to books geared to a museum's topic you'll find reproduction furnishings and decorative arts, jewellery, and apparel related to the museum's collection. The Smithsonian is Washington's third-largest retailer. The Hirshhorn Museum offers modern jewellery; the National Museum of American History has reproduction 19th-century toys, kitchenware, and quilts; the Corcoran offers blown-glass objects and woven scarves; the Building Museum sells tools and architectural puzzles; there are bonsai pots in the National Arboretum; the latest stamps at the National Postal Museum; and freeze-dried ice cream at the National Air and Space Museum.

AMBIANCE GALLERIES

These well-appointed galleries place emphasis on one-of-a-kind accessories, including sculpture, fine art, porcelain, furniture, and lighting.
D3 1647 Wisconsin Avenue NW 202/944-4007 Mon–Sat 11–5 Foggy Bottom, then bus No. 34

THE AMERICAN HAND

This gallery-shop sells one-of-a-kind and limited-edition international ceramics, textiles, and wood crafts for home and office.
E3 2906 M Street NW 202/965-3273 Mon–Sat 11–6; Sun 1–5 Farragut West, then bus No. 32

APPALACHIAN SPRING

Seek this out for ceramics, quilts, fine woodwork, and other traditional and contemporary crafts. Also has a branch in Union Station.
D3 1415 Wisconsin Avenue NW 202/337-5780 Mon–Sat 10–9; Sun noon–5 Farragut West, then bus No. 32

CANAL SQUARE GALLERIES

Works include central and eastern European art, contemporary Asian artists, and modern realism in these three separate galleries under one roof.
D3 3112 M Street NW 202/338-6456 Tue–Sat noon–6 Foggy Bottom, then bus No. 34

CHENONCEAU ANTIQUES

American 19th- and 20th-century antiques, and mission oak are chosen here by someone with a sophisticated knowledge of this period.
F2 2314 18th Street NW 202/667-1651 Sat, Sun 12–6.30 Dupont Circle, then bus No. 42

CHERISHABLES

The emphasis here is on 18th-century Federal furniture and decorations.
F3 1608 20th Street NW 202/785-4087 Mon–Sat 11–6 Dupont Circle

DISCOVERY CHANNEL STORE

Four-level store selling unique products from around the world designed to educate and entertain.
H4 MCI Center, 601 F Street NW 202/639-0908 Mon–Sat 10–7; Sun 12–6 Gallery Place-Chinatown

GALLERIES OF DUPONT CIRCLE

Fine contemporary and older art from around the world are on offer in 22 independent galleries.
F3 1710 Connecticut Avenue NW 202/328-7189 Tue–Sat 11–5 Dupont Circle

GEORGETOWN ANTIQUES CENTER

Victorian art nouveau and art deco objects are displayed in an accommodating Victorian town house.
E3 2918 M Street NW 202/338-3811 Mon–Sat 11–6; Sun 12–5 Foggy Bottom

G. K. S. BUSH

Browse among early American high-style furniture and related art.

E3 2828 Pennsylvania Avenue NW 202/965-0653 Mon–Fri 10–6; Sat 10–5 Foggy Bottom

INDIAN CRAFT SHOP
This shop showcases hand-crafted Eskimo walrus-ivory carving, Zuni pots, Hopi dolls, and Navajo pottery.
F5 Department of Interior, 1849 C Street NW, Room 1023 202/208-4056 Mon–Fri 8.30–4.30 Farragut West

KEITH LIPERT GALLERY
American and European decorative art from contemporary designers.
E3 2922 M Street NW 202/965-9736 Mon–Sat 11–6; Sun 1–5 Foggy Bottom

MARSTON LUCE
American folk art, weather-vanes, and geometric textiles line the shelves.
F5 1314 21st Street NW 202/775-9460 Mon–Sat 11–6 Farragut West, then bus No. 42

MAURINE LITTLETON GALLERY
Specializes in sculptured glass by modern designers, including American Dale Chihuly.
D3 1667 Wisconsin Avenue NW 202/333-9307 Tue–Sat 11–6 Foggy Bottom, then bus No. 32 or 36

MILLENNIUM DECORATIVE ARTS
Furniture, accessories, clothing, and books from 1940 to 1970, along with new products inspired by the styles of the period.
G2 1528 U Street NW 202/483-1218 Thu–Sun noon–7 U Street-Cardozo

THE PHOENIX
This is the place to come for Mexican folk crafts, silver jewellery, and natural-fibre native and contemporary clothing.
D3 1514 Wisconsin Avenue NW 202/338-4404 Mon–Sat 10–6; Sun 11–5 Farragut West, then bus No. 35

RETROSPECTIVE
Retrospective sells the things baby-boomers grew up on in the 1940s and 1950s: streamlined designs in metal furniture, clunky tableware, and bold patterns.
F2 2324 18th Street NW 202/483-8112 Mon, Wed–Fri noon–7; Sat 11–7; Sun 12–6 Dupont Circle, then bus No. 42

SARAH WESSEL DESIGN
A town house full of unusual items including antiques, decorative objects, and furnishings.
D3 3214 O Street NW 202/337-1910 Mon–Sat 11–5.30 Foggy Bottom, then bus No. 36

SUSQUEHANNA
Susquehanna specializes in American and English furniture and works of art in the largest antique space in Georgetown.
D3 3216 O Street NW 202/333-1511 Mon–Sat 10–6 Foggy Bottom, then bus No. 35

SWISS WATCH WORKS
Classic and vintage pocket or wrist watches.
D3 1512 Wisconsin Avenue NW 202/333-4550 Tue–Fri 10–7; Sat 10–6 Foggy Bottom, then bus No. 32

VINTAGE SECOND-HAND SHOPPING

The dedicated shopper with an eye for style–but not necessarily at high-street prices–can browse in Washington's second-hand shops. Check out: **Once Is Not Enough** for used but stylish men's, women's, and children's clothing and accessories (A2 4830 MacArthur Boulevard NW 202/337-3072 Mon–Sat 10–5 Metro Center, then bus No. D6); **The Opportunity Shop of the Christ Child Society** for vintage clothing, housewares, and antiques (D3 1427 Wisconsin Avenue NW 202/ 333-6635 Tue–Sat 10–3.45 Farragut West, then bus No. 32); and **Secondi** for women's fashions from Gap to Chanel (F3 1702 Connecticut Avenue NW 202/667-1122 Mon–Sat 11–6; Sun 1–5 Dupont Circle).

Books & Music

BOOKS FOR NIGHT OWLS

You can find bookstores open well into the night in nearly every area of Washington, many with cafés, knowledgeable staff, and discounts. There is always a place to browse. Kramerbooks & Afterwords Café (see main entry this page) is open 24 hours each Saturday and Sunday.

BIRD-IN-HAND BOOKSTORE AND GALLERY
Located in a historic Capital Hill house, this shop specializes in art, architecture, and design.
K6 323 7th Street SE 202/543-0744 Tue–Sat 10–5 Eastern Market

BOOKS A MILLION
This new chain specializes in bestsellers, crafts, popular psychology, fiction, and the "kiss'n'tell" books so beloved of Washington scandal-mongers. Everything is heavily discounted.
F3 11 Dupont Circle NW 202/319-1374 Daily 9AM–11PM Dupont Circle

BORDERS BOOKS AND MUSIC
This spacious outlet of the national chain offers 325,000 titles (including 50,000 music titles) plus a café, readings, signings, and events.
F3 18th and L Streets NW 202/466-4999 Mon–Thu 8AM–9PM; Fri 8AM–10PM Sat 8AM–9PM Farragut West

CHAPTERS LITERARY BOOKSTORE
Specializing in poetry, fiction, and literary criticism, Chapters takes books seriously.
F3 1512 K Street NW 202/347-5495 Mon–Fri 10–6.30; Sat 11–5 McPherson Square

KEMP MILL MUSIC
This local chain keeps prices low on a full range of CDs and tapes.
F2 2459 18th Street NW 202/387-1011 Mon–Fri 8.30AM–9PM; Sat 10–7; Sun 12–5 (both branches) Dupont Circle F4 1900 L Street NW 202/223-5310 Farragut West

KRAMERBOOKS & AFTERWORDS CAFÉ
The quintessential Washington literary pick-up scene and one of the city's oldest booksellers.
F4 1517 Connecticut Avenue NW 202/387-1400 Sat, Sun 24 hours; Mon–Fri 7.30AM–1AM Dupont Circle

LAMBDA RISING BOOKSTORE
Gay and lesbian books and gifts.
E3 1625 Connecticut Avenue NW 202/462-6969 Daily 10AM–midnight Dupont Circle

LAMMAS WOMEN'S BOOKSTORE & MORE
Books by and for women.
E3 1607 17th Street NW 202/775-8218 Mon–Thu, Sat 11–10; Sun 11–8 Dupont Circle

MELODY RECORD SHOP
Knowledgeable staff and a 10–40 percent discount on CDs and cassettes.
F3 1623 Connecticut Avenue NW 202/232-4002 Mon–Thu 10–10; Fri–Sat 10AM–11PM; Sun 11–10 Farragut North, Dupont Circle

MYSTERYBOOKS
Specializes in puzzle books and a wide range of mystery publications.
F3 1715 Connecticut Avenue NW 202/483-1600 Mon–Fri 11–7; Sat 10–6; Sun noon–5

OLSSON'S BOOKS & RECORDS
The comprehensive stock covers most areas of publishing. Folk and classical recordings come in many formats.
D3 1239 Wisconsin Avenue NW 202/338-9544 Mon–Thu 10AM–11PM; Fri–Sat 10AM–midnight; Sun 11–10 Farragut West, then bus No. 32

ORPHEUS RECORDS
All styles of music in most formats. Vinyl hunters come for the good used LPs as well as the best selection of new vinyl in the metropolitan area.
A5 3173 Wilson Boulevard, Arlington, VA 703/294-6774 Mon–Sat noon–11; Sun noon–8 Clarendon

POLITICS AND PROSE
The area's largest independent bookstore has comfortable reading chairs, a coffee shop, and knowledgeable staff.
Off map at E1 5015 Connecticut Avenue NW 202/364-1919 Sun–Thu 9AM–10.30PM; Fri, Sat 9–9 VanNess, then a 15minute walk north

SECOND STORY BOOKS
If used books are your passion, start here. If you don't find your treasure on the lines of shelves, it may be in Second Story's warehouse.
F3 2000 P Street NW 202/659-8884 Daily 10–10 Dupont Circle

SISTER'S SPACE & BOOKS
Books by and about African-American women are the focus here.
G2 1515 U Street NW 202/332-3433 Mon–Sat 10–7; Sun noon–5 U Street-Cardozo

TOWER RECORDS
Loud and hip, Tower has the largest selection of cassettes and CDs in Washington.
E4 2000 Pennsylvania Avenue NW 202/331-2400 Daily 9AM–midnight Foggy Bottom

TRAVEL BOOKS & LANGUAGE
TB&L has been called the Library of Congress of travel-book stores, stocking the nation's largest selection of maps, classic and historical travel literature, architectural and destination guides. You'll find 140 languages and dialects represented and many cultural events are on offer.
Off map at C1 4437 Wisconsin Avenue NW 202/237-1322; 800/220-2665 Mon–Sat 10–10; Sun noon–7 America U-Tenley Town

US GOVERNMENT BOOKSTORE
On hand here are the countless publications produced by the Feds, including research reports on a huge range of subjects.
G4 1510 H Street NW 202/653-5075 Mon–Fri 8.30–4.30 McPherson Square

VERTIGO BOOKS
Specializes in African-American as well as international writers.
F3 1337 Connecticut Avenue, NW 202/429-9272 Mon–Fri 10–7; Sat 11–7; Sun 12–5 Dupont Circle

SPECIAL-INTEREST TOMES

Specialist books can be located at the headquarters of the the hundreds of professional associations, think tanks, and foundations that make Washington home–the Brookings Institution, the Carnegie Endowment for International Peace, the Freedom Forum, the American Association of Museums, the American Institute of Architects, and even the American Society of Association Executives. If you've got an interest in architecture, bee-keeping, chemistry, or zoology, you can find both popular and scholarly editions for your passion.

Live Music & Comedy Clubs

NIGHT OPTIONS

Washington clubs offer every kind of music. You can have it live or played by a DJ. You can dance or just listen. Or check out one of the murder mystery dinners, whodunnits where the audience gets involved with the story while watching it. The **Blair Mansion Inn** (✉ 7711 Eastern Avenue, Silver Spring, MD ☎ 301/588-6646) and **Murder Upon Request** (✉ Old Arlington Hilton Hotel, 950 N Stafford Street, Arlington ☎ 703/379-8108) have weekend shows.

LIVE MUSIC

9:30 CLUB

This trendy club is hot in summer, cold in winter, and always dark and smoky, but you can't beat it for local, national, and international progressive music.

✚ G4 ✉ 815 V Street NW ☎ 202/393-0930 ⏲ Generally Sun–Thu 7.30PM–midnight; Fri, Sat 9PM–2AM Ⓜ Metro Center ✋ Cover charge. Tickets at the door or from TicketMaster

BIRCHMERE

The best place in the area to hear national acoustic folk and bluegrass acts, plus occasional rockabilly or rock.

✚ Off map at E10 ✉ 3701 Mount Vernon Avenue, Alexandria, VA ☎ 703/549-7500 ⏲ Sun–Thu 6.30PM–11PM; Fri, Sat 7PM–12.30AM

BLUES ALLEY

Washington's best jazz club serves up national jazz acts, such as Ramsey Lewis and Charlie Byrd. The Creole cooking is not bad either.

✚ D3 ✉ Rear 1073 Wisconsin Avenue NW ☎ 202/337-4141 ⏲ Sun–Thu 6PM–midnight; Fri, Sat 6PM–2AM. Shows at 8 and 10, plus occasional midnight shows Fri and Sat Ⓜ Farragut West, then bus No. 32 or 38B ✋ Cover charge and minimum charge

THE GARAGE

This club hosts a wide variety of bands, from alternative and traditional rock to blues, reggae, and hip-hop.

✚ F3 ✉ 1214 18th Street NW ☎ 202/331-7123 ⏲ Open when there is a show, usually until 1AM Ⓜ Dupont Circle

METRO CAFE

Usually features newer, alternative-type rock acts; also occasional films and theatre performances.

✚ G3 ✉ 1522 14th Street NW ✉ 202/518-7900 ⏲ Mon–Thu 7PM–2AM; Fri, Sat 7PM–3AM; Sun 7PM–2AM Ⓜ Dupont Circle

MURPHY'S

With a name like Murphy's you know it's going to be Irish music. Live music isn't nightly, so call ahead.

✚ E4 ✉ 2609 24th Street NW ☎ 202/462-7171 ⏲ Sun–Thu 11AM–1.30AM; Fri, Sat 11AM–2.30AM Ⓜ Foggy Bottom

ONE STEP DOWN

Smoky, low-ceilinged, and intimate like all good jazz clubs. It also has the best jazz jukebox in town. Local acts and New York jazz artists live Wednesday to Saturday.

✚ E4 ✉ 2517 Pennsylvania Avenue NW ☎ 202/955-7141 ⏲ Mon–Thu 10AM–2AM; Fri 10AM–3AM; Sat noon–3AM; Sun noon–2AM Ⓜ Foggy Bottom ✋ Cover charge and minimum charge

COMEDY

CAPITOL STEPS

Political musical revues, weekends at various venues.

☎ 703/683-8330

GROSS NATIONAL PRODUCT

Political satire on Saturdays at Chief Ike's.

✚ F1 ✉ 1725 Columbia Road NW ☎ 202/783-7212 ⏲ Mon–Thu 4PM–2AM; Fri 4PM–3AM; Sat noon–3AM; Sun 4PM–2AM Ⓜ Dupont Circle, then bus No. 42

Bars & Lounges

BRICKSKELLER

With more than 800 brands of beer, from Central American lagers to US microbrews, this is Washington's premier pub. Bartenders oblige beer-can collectors by opening the containers from the bottom.

E3 · 1523 22nd Street NW · 202/293-1885 · Mon–Thu 11.30AM–2AM; Fri 11.30AM–3AM; Sat 6AM–3AM; Sun 6PM–2AM · Dupont Circle

CAPITOL CITY BREWING COMPANY

This microbrewery, the first brewery in Washington since Prohibition, makes everything from a bitter to a bock, though not all types are available at all times. At the gleaming copper bar, metal steps lead up to the brewing tanks. A second branch is to be found inside the Postal Museum building near Union Station.

G4 · 1100 New York Avenue NW · 202/628-2222 · Mon–Sat 11AM–2AM; Sun 11AM–midnight · Metro Center
J4 · 2 Massachusetts Avenue NE · 202/842-2337 · Daily lunch, dinner · Union Station

CHAMPIONS

In one of DC's biggest sports bars, the walls are covered with jerseys, pucks, bats, and balls, and the big game of the evening is always showing on the big screen.

D3 · 1206 Wisconsin Avenue NW · 202/965-4005 · Mon–Thu 5AM–2AM; Fri 5PM–3AM; Sat 11.30AM–3AM; Sun 11.30AM–2AM. One-drink minimum Fri and Sat after 10PM · Farragut West, then bus No. 32

THE DUBLINER

The closest thing in Washington to an Irish pub, this is a favourite with Capitol Hill staffers.

J4 · 520 N Capitol Street NW · 202/737-3773 · Sun–Thu 11AM–1.30AM; Fri, Sat 11AM–2.30AM · Union Station

HAWK'N'DOVE

A friendly neighbourhood bar, frequented by political types, lobbyists, and Marines (from the nearby barracks).

J6 · 329 Pennsylvania Avenue SE · 202/543-3300 · Sun–Thu 10AM–2AM; Fri, Sat 10AM–3AM · Capitol South

OZIO

One of Washington's first cigar-and-martini bars, Ozio still attracts K Street lawyers and lobbyists.

F4 · 1835 K Street NW · 202/822-6000 · Sun–Thu noon–2AM; Fri, Sat noon–3AM · Farragut North or Farragut West

SIGN OF THE WHALE

Well-known postpreppie/neoyuppie haven right in the heart of a densely bar-populated area downtown.

F3 · 1825 M Street NW · 202/785-1110 · Sun–Thu 11.30AM–2AM; Fri, Sat 11.30AM–3AM · Farragut North

YACHT CLUB

Just across the city limits in Maryland, this lounge is popular with well-dressed, middle-aged singles. Jacket and tie or turtleneck required (casual Wednesday).

Off map at C1 · 8111 Woodmont Avenue, Bethesda, MD · 301/654-2396 · Tue–Thu 5PM–1AM; Fri 5PM–2AM; Sat 8AM–2AM.

WHERE THE ACTION IS

Washington has pockets of activity downtown and in its more ethnically diverse neighbourhoods. Adams-Morgan, around 18th Street and Columbia Road, has many bars, clubs, and restaurants. Capitol Hill (especially along Pennsylvania Avenue SE), the U Street NW corridor (from about 14th Street to 18th Street), and the downtown area (around 19th and M Streets NW), are also fairly dense with night-time activities.

Theatres

TICKETS

Buy tickets in person at the Old Post Office Pavilion (☒ 1100 Pennsylvania Avenue NW ⊙ Tue–Sat 11–6). Tickets for Sunday and Monday performances are sold on Saturday. There is a 10 percent service charge per order. Tickets to most events are sold by three main ticket outlets as well as by the box office. **TicketMaster** (☎ 202/432-7328) sells tickets by phone and at some stores, including Hecht and Company, to concerts, sports events, and many special events. **Protix** (☎ 703/218-6500) has tickets to shows at Wolf Trap and some other venues. **TicketPlace** (☎ 202/842-5387) sells half-price, day-of-performance tickets for selected shows (it is also a full-price TicketMaster outlet).

ARENA STAGE

Arena manages a long season in its three theatres: the theatre-in-the-round Arena, the proscenium Kreeger, and the cabaret-style Old Vat Room. The New Voices series offers the chance to see new plays in development at reduced prices.
✚ H7 ☒ 6th Street and Maine Avenue SW ☎ 202/488-3300 Ⓜ Waterfront

FORD'S THEATER

The theatre where President Abraham Lincoln was assassinated now mostly mounts musicals (Dickens's *A Christmas Carol* is presented every December).
✚ G4 ☒ 511 10th Street NW ☎ 202/347-4833 Ⓜ Metro Center

GALA HISPANIC THEATER

Spanish classics as well as contemporary and modern Latin-American plays in both Spanish and English.
✚ Off map at F1 ☒ 1625 Park Road NW ☎ 202/234-7174 Dupont Circle, then bus No. 42

NATIONAL THEATER

Destroyed by fire and rebuilt four times, the National Theater has operated in the same location since 1835. It presents pre- and post-Broadway shows.
✚ G4 ☒ 1321 Pennsylvania Avenue NW ☎ 202/628-6161 Ⓜ Metro Center

SHAKESPEARE THEATER

The season here includes five plays, three by the Bard and two by other playwrights.
✚ H5 ☒ 450 7th Street NW ☎ 202/547-1122 Ⓜ Archives-Navy Memorial

SIGNATURE THEATER

The five-play season ranges from contemporary renditions of classics and musicals to new drama.
✚ B10 ☒ 3806 South Four Mile Run Drive, Arlington, VA ☎ 703/218-6500 Ⓜ Pentagon, then bus No. 22A, 22B or 22C

SOURCE THEATER

The 107-seat Source Theater presents established plays and modern interpretations of classics. Each July and August, Source hosts a series of new plays, many by local playwrights.
✚ G2 ☒ 1835 14th Street NW ☎ 202/462–1073 Ⓜ U Street-Cardozo

STUDIO THEATER

One of Washington's nicest independent company theatres, Studio performs classics and offbeat plays. The 50-seat Secondstage mounts experimental works.
✚ G3 ☒ 1333 P Street NW ☎ 202/332-3300 Ⓜ Dupont Circle

WARNER THEATER

Theatre and dance performances, as well as some pop music shows.
✚ G4 ☒ 13th and E Streets NW ☎ 202/783-4000 Ⓜ Metro Center

WOOLLY MAMMOTH THEATER COMPANY

Experimental and contemporary plays.
✚ G3 ☒ 1401 Church Street NW ☎ 202/393-3939 Ⓜ Dupont Circle

Concert Venues

DAR CONSTITUTION HALL

Formerly home of the National Symphony Orchestra, this 3,700-seat hall hosts musical performances, staged shows, and occasional big-name comedy acts.
F5 18th and D Streets NW 202/638-2661 Farragut West, then walk six blocks south)

GEORGE MASON UNIVERSITY

The GMU campus in suburban Virginia is home to the Center for the Arts. The Patriot Center, also on campus, holds concerts and sporting events.
Off map at A2 Route 123 and Braddock Road, Fairfax, VA Center for the Arts 703/993-8888; Patriot Center 703/993-3000 or 202/432-7328

LISNER AUDITORIUM

This 1,500-seat theatre, on the George Washington University campus, presents pop, classical, and choral concerts.
F4 21st and H Streets NW 202/994-1500 Foggy Bottom

MERRIWEATHER POST PAVILION

An hour north of DC, this outdoor pavilion with covered seating hosts big-name acts in summer.
Off map at M1 10475 Little Patuxent Parkway, Columbia, MD 301/982-1800; tickets 703/218-6500

NATIONAL GALLERY OF ART

The National Gallery Orchestra, and guest recitalists and ensembles, hold free concerts in the West Building's West Garden Court on Sunday evenings from October to June.
H5 6th Street and Constitution Avenue NW 202/842-6941 Archives-Navy Memorial

NISSAN PAVILION AT STONE RIDGE

This 25,000-seat venue near Manassas hosts rock, country, and pop concerts.
Off map at A5 7800 Cellar Door Drive, Gainesville, VA 703/754-6400 or 202/432-7328

SMITHSONIAN INSTITUTION

An assortment of music—both free and ticketed—at various locations. The Smithsonian Associates Program (202/357-3030) offers everything from a cappella groups to Cajun zydeco bands.
G5, H5, H4 At various Smithsonian museums, most of which are on the Mall 202/357-2700 Smithsonian

MCI CENTER

The 20,000-seat home of Washington's pro basketball and hockey teams also has regular pop concerts.
H4 601 F Street NW, Information 202/628-3200; tickets 202/432-7328 Gallery Place, Chinatown

WOLF TRAP FARM PARK

About a 20-minute drive from Washington, you can picnic in the national park before taking in an opera, dance or concert.
Off map at A2 1624 Trap Road, Vienna VA Information 703/255-1900; tickets 703/255-1860

JOHN F. KENNEDY CENTER FOR THE PERFORMING ARTS

The John F. Kennedy Center (➤ 27) is indeed a centre for cultural events, with five separate stages under one roof: the Concert Hall, home to the National Symphony Orchestra; the Opera House, for ballet, modern dance, opera, and large-scale musicals; the Eisenhower Theater, usually used for drama; the Terrace Theater, a smaller stage for chamber groups and experimental works; and the Theater Lab.

AMERICAN FOLKLIFE

The Smithsonian's Festival of American Folklife provides an alternative to high culture and fine art. Each year the Smithsonian celebrates one country, one state, one profession, and a number of musical folk traditions. Summer temperatures persuade bureaucrats and others to join in early evening, open-air dance parties.

The Performing Arts & Movies

MOVIES

Check the daily newspapers for mainstream first-run movies–theatres are scattered throughout the city. For less mainstream first-run and foreign films, try the **Cineplex Odeon** theatres such as Dupont Circle, Inner Circle of Janus 3 (☎ 202/333-FILM, which translates to 3456). For revivals and foreign, independent, and avant-garde films, try the **American Film Institute** (✉ Kennedy Center ☎ 202/785-4600). **The Hirshhorn Museum** (☎ 202/357-2700), National Gallery of Art East Building (☎ 202/737-4215), and **National Archives** (☎ 202/501-5000), all on the Mall, often show historical, unusual, or experimental films. The **Library of Congress** (☎ 202/707-5677) often shows old movies, including some silent films. **Filmfest DC** (☎ 202/274-6810), an annual citywide festival of international cinema, takes place in late April and early May.

CHAMBER MUSIC

CORCORAN GALLERY OF ART

F4–F5 ✉ 17th Street and New York Avenue NW ☎ 202/639-1700 Periodically throughout the year

FOLGER SHAKESPEARE LIBRARY

The Folger Consort plays medieval, Renaissance, and baroque music.
J5 ✉ 201 East Capitol Street SE ☎ 202/544-7077 Oct–May

NATIONAL ACADEMY OF SCIENCES

E5 ✉ 2101 Constitution Avenue NW ☎ 202/334-2436 Oct–May Free

PHILLIPS COLLECTION

F3 ✉ 1600 21st Street NW ☎ 202/387-2151 Sep–May: Sun 5pm

CONCERT SERIES

ARMED FORCES CONCERT SERIES

The Capitol's East Terrace and the Sylvan Theater near the Washington Monument.
☎ Air Force 202/767-5658; Army 703/696-3399; Navy 202/433-2525; Marines 202/433-4011 Jun–Aug: Mon–Fri evenings

CARTER BARRON AMPHITHEATER

Pop, jazz, and gospel music. The Shakespeare Theater (➤ 82) presents a free play outdoors in June.
Off map at F1 ✉ 16th Street and Colorado Avenue NW ☎ 202/426-0486 Mid-Jun to Aug: Sat, Sun

CHORAL GROUPS

CHORAL ARTS SOCIETY

A 180-voice choir performs at the John F. Kennedy Center (➤ 27).
Periodically throughout the year, plus three Christmas sing-alongs

WASHINGTON NATIONAL CATHEDRAL

Choral and church groups (➤ 61).

SHRINE OF THE IMMACULATE CONCEPTION

Venue for choral groups (➤ 49).

DANCE

DANCE PLACE

Modern and ethnic dance.
Off map at K1 ✉ 3225 8th Street NE ☎ 202/269-1600 Sat, Sun

JOY OF MOTION

Home to area troupes.
Off map at C1 ✉ 1643 Connecticut Avenue NW ☎ 202/387-0911

MOUNT VERNON COLLEGE

Hosts visiting dance companies, fall and spring.
B2 ✉ 2100 Foxhall Road NW ☎ 202/625-4655

THE SMITHSONIAN ASSOCIATES PROGRAM

Dance groups perform at Smithsonian museums.
☎ 202/357-3030

THE WASHINGTON BALLET

Ballet performances, plus *The Nutcracker* in December ☎ 202/362-3606

Sports

BIKING

WASHINGTON AREA BICYCLIST ASSOCIATION
Information on bike trails in and around Washington.
✉ 818 Connecticut Avenue NW, Suite 300, 20006 ☎ 202/628-2500

Some of the best rides are along the George Washington Memorial Parkway, along the Virginia side of the Potomac River to Mount Vernon (56km (35mi) round trip); the C & O Canal towpath from Georgetown to Cumberland, MD (290km (180mi) one way); and through Rock Creek Park. Rent bicycles from:

BICYCLE PRO SHOP
✉ 3403 M Street NW Boulevard, Alexandria, VA ☎ 202/337-0311

BIG WHEEL BIKES
✉ 1034 33rd Street NW, Georgetown ☎ 202/337-0254

CITY BIKES
✉ 2501 Champlain Street NW
☎ 202/265-1564

DISTRICT HARDWARE
✉ 2003 P Street NW
☎ 202/659-8686

METROPOLIS BICYCLES
Also rents rollerblades.
✉ 709 8th Street SE, Capitol Hill
☎ 202/543-8900

BOATING

FLETCHER'S BOAT HOUSE
Rowboats, canoes, and bicycles for rent.
✉ C & O Canal towpath, 3.2km (2mi) north of Georgetown, near Reservoir Road NW
☎ 202/244-0461

THOMPSON'S BOAT CENTER
Rents canoes, rowboats, rowing shells, sailboards, and bicycles.
✉ Virginia Avenue and Rock Creek Park, behind Kennedy Center ☎ 202/333-4861

Paddle boats are available in summer on the east side of the Tidal Basin in front of the Jefferson Memorial.
☎ 202/479-2426

GOLF

Washington has three public golf courses:

HAINS POINT
✉ East Potomac Park near the Jefferson Memorial
☎ 202/554-7660

LANGSTON GOLF COURSE
✉ 26th Street and Benning Road NE ☎ 202/397-8638

ROCK CREEK PARK
✉ 16th and Rittenhouse Streets NW ☎ 202/882-7332

In the suburbs:

RESTON NATIONAL
✉ 11875 Sunrise Valley Drive, Reston, VA ☎ 703/620-9333

NORTHWEST PARK
✉ 15701 Layhill Road, Wheaton, MD ☎ 301/598-6100

TENNIS

The District of Columbia has 144 outdoor courts.
✉ Department of Recreation, 3149 16th Street NW, 20010
☎ 202/673-7646

SPECTATOR SPORTS

If you are here in autumn, you will hear about the Redskins American football team, but season-ticket holders have all the seats. You'll have better luck seeing the Wizards play basketball or the Capitals play hockey, both at the MCI Center in downtown Washington. For tickets, call TicketMaster (➤ 82).

Luxury Hotels

HOTEL PRICES

Expect to pay the following prices per night for a double room (excluding 13 percent tax–9.75 percent in Virginia–plus $1.50 per night occupancy tax):

Budget **up to $150**
Mid-range **up to $250**
Luxury **more than $250**

When you make your reservation it's always worth asking whether any special deals are available.

BOOKING AGENCIES

Capitol Reservations
Books rooms at over 70 hotels at 20–40 percent off certain rates ☎ 202/452-1270 or 800/847-4832 ⌚ Mon–Fri 8.30–6.30

Washington DC Accommodations
Books rooms in any hotel in town, with discounts of 20–40 percent available at about 40 locations ☎ 202/289-2220 or 800/554-2220 ⌚ Mon–Fri 9–6

FOUR SEASONS HOTEL
On the eastern edge of Georgetown, this hotel is known as a gathering place for Washington's elite.
E3 ✉ 2800 Pennsylvania Avenue NW ☎ 202/342-0444 or 800/332-3442, fax 202/944-2076 Foggy Bottom

HAY-ADAMS HOTEL
Looking like a mansion on the outside and an English country house within, this hotel has a picture-postcard White House view—ask for a room on the south side.
F4 ✉ 800 16th Street NW ☎ 202/638-6600 or 800/233-6800, fax 202/638-2716 McPherson Square

JEFFERSON HOTEL
Small luxury hotel done up in Federal style; outstanding service.
F3 ✉ 1200 16th Street NW ☎ 202/347-2200 or 800/235-6397, fax 202/331-7982 Farragut North

PARK HYATT
A notable collection of modern art adorns this hotel. Reproductions of Chinese antiques accent the rooms, a mix of traditional and contemporary styles.
E3 ✉ 1201 24th Street NW ☎ 202/789-1234 or 800/233-1234, fax 202/419-6795 Foggy Bottom

RITZ-CARLTON, PENTAGON CITY
Public spaces in this hotel display a $2-million art and antiques collection. Many guest rooms have a view of the monuments across the Potomac River.
D8 ✉ 1250 S Hayes Street Arlington, VA ☎ 703/415-5000 or 800/241-3333, fax 703/415-5061 Pentagon City

STOUFFER RENAISSANCE MAYFLOWER
The ornate lobby glistens with gilded trim and the rooms feature custom-designed furniture.
F4 ✉ 1127 Connecticut Avenue NW ☎ 202/347-3000 or 800/228-9290, fax 202/776-9182 Farragut North

SWISSOTEL WASHINGTON, THE WATERGATE
Best known for its part in the fall of Richard Nixon, this hotel has large rooms, most with river views and many with balconies.
E4 ✉ 2650 Virginia Avenue NW ☎ 202/965-2300 or 800/424-2736, fax 202/337-7915 Foggy Bottom

WESTIN FAIRFAX
Lovely hotel with European furnishings and 18th- and 19th-century English art.
F3 ✉ 2100 Massachusetts Avenue NW ☎ 202/293-2100 or 800/325-3535, fax 202/835-2196 Dupont Circle

WILLARD INTER-CONTINENTAL
Heads of state have made the Willard, steps from the White House, home since 1853. The lobby is Beaux Arts, the rooms quite plain.
G4 ✉ 1401 Pennsylvania Avenue NW ☎ 202/628-9100 or 800/327-0200, fax 202/637-7326 McPherson Square

Mid-Range Hotels

CAPITOL HILL SUITES
This apartment hotel is tucked away behind the Madison Building of the Library of Congress.
J6 200 C Street SE 202/543-6000 or 800/424-9165, fax 202/547-2608 Capitol South

DOUBLETREE GUEST SUITES
Both of these apartment hotels are close to Georgetown and the John F. Kennedy Center.
E4 801 New Hampshire Avenue NW 202/785-2000 or 800/222-8733, fax 202/785-9485) Foggy Bottom
E4 2500 Pennsylvania Avenue NW 202/333-8060 or 800/222-8733, fax 202/338-3818 Foggy Bottom

HENLEY PARK HOTEL
A bit of Britain in a developing neighbourhood, this is a National Trust for Historic Preservation designated Historic Hotel.
G4 926 Massachusetts Avenue NW 202/638-5200 or 800/222-8474, fax 202/638-6740 Metro Center/Gallery Place

HOTEL WASHINGTON
Well-known for its view, this lovely hotel is just a block from the White House, which you can see from the rooftop Sky Terrace from May through October.
G4 515 15th Street NW 202/638-5900 or 800/424-9540, fax 202/638-4275 Metro Center

HOTEL MONTICELLO
This homey, apartment hotel is on a side street in Georgetown.
D4 1075 Thomas Jefferson Street NW 202/337-0900 or 800/388-2410, fax 202/ 333-6526

LATHAM HOTEL
This small, colonial-style hotel on one of Georgetown's main streets offers views of busy M Street or the C & O Canal. Its Citronelle restaurant is one of Washington's best.
D3 3000 M Street NW 202/726-5000 or 800/528-4261, fax 202/337-4250

MORRISON-CLARK INN HOTEL
Created by merging two 1864 town houses, this inn is another of the National Trust for Historic Preservation designated Historic Hotels. The restaurant is well regarded.
G4 1015 L Street NW 202/898-1200 or 800/332-7898, fax 202/289-8576 Mount Vernon Square-UDC

NORMANDY INN
This European-style hotel is on a quiet street in the exclusive Connecticut Avenue embassy area. There is a wine and cheese reception every Tuesday evening.
E2 2118 Wyoming Avenue NW 202/483-1350 or 800/423-6953, fax 202/387-8241

RIVER INN
This small, all-suite hotel is near Georgetown, George Washington University, and the John F. Kennedy Center. Rooms are homey if modest.
E4 924 25th Street NW 202/337-7600 or 800/424-2741, fax 202/337-6520 Foggy Bottom

WASHINGTON HOTELS

Most major chains have hotels in the city and the nearby suburbs. For a complete list of hotels, contact the Washington, DC, Convention and Visitors Association (1212 New York Avenue NW, Washington, DC, 20005 202/789-7000). All the hotels here are air-conditioned. Nearly all the finer hotels have superb restaurants whose traditionally high prices are almost always completely justified.

Budget Accommodations

BED & BREAKFAST

To find reasonably priced accommodations in small guest houses and private homes, contact either of the following bed-and-breakfast services: **Bed 'n' Breakfast Accommodations Ltd.** of Washington, DC, (✉ Box 12011, Washington, DC, 20005 ☎ 202/328-3510); or **Bed and Breakfast League Ltd.** (✉ Box 9490, Washington, DC, 20016-9490 ☎ 202/363-7767). If you require a private bath, make it clear when you book.

BEST WESTERN DOWNTOWN CAPITOL HILL

Furnished in typical chain budget-hotel fashion, this is located near several tourist sites, including the National Archives, Union Station, the National Gallery of Art, and Chinatown .
H4 ✉ 724 Third Street NW ☎ 202/842-4466 or 800/528-1254, fax 202/842-4831 Judiciary Square

DAYS INN CONNECTICUT AVENUE

Standard hotel away from downtown, but only two blocks from the Metro.
Off map at E1 ✉ 4400 Connecticut Avenue NW ☎ 202/244-5600 or 800/329-7466, fax 202/244-6794 Van Ness

HOLIDAY INN EISENHOWER

A bargain for the budget traveller, near Old Town in Alexandria.
Off map at E10 ✉ 2460 Eisenhower Avenue, Alexandria, VA ☎ 703/960-3400 or 800/465-4329, fax 703/329-0953 Eisenhower

HOSTELING INTERNATIONAL WASHINGTON, DC

Well-kept hostel with bunk-bedded dormitory rooms; families may get their own rooms if the hostel is not full.
G4 ✉ 1009 11th Street NW ☎ 202/737-2333, fax 202/737-1508 McPherson Square

HOTEL HARRINGTON

This is your basic clean, no-frills hotel, but with a great location. The Mall and many museums are just a few blocks away.
G4 ✉ 436 11th Street NW ☎ 202/628-8140 or 800/424-8532, fax 202/347-3924 Metro Center

HOTEL TABARD INN

Three Victorian town houses joined together. Charmingly well-worn furnishings.
F3 ✉ 1739 N Street NW ☎ 202/785-1277, fax 202/785-6173 Dupont Circle

HOWARD JOHNSON'S EXPRESS INN

On one of the main routes into the city.
K3 ✉ 600 New York Avenue NE ☎ 202/546-9200 or 800/446-4656, fax 202/546-6348 Rhode Island, then bus No. P6

KALORAMA GUEST HOUSE

Five separate early 20th-century town houses, decorated with old-fashioned charm. There are no phones or TVs (except in suites), but breakfast and afternoon aperitifs are included.
F2 ✉ 1854 Mintwood Place NW ☎ 202/667-6369, fax 202/319-1262 Woodley Park-Zoo
E1 ✉ 2700 Cathedral Avenue NW ☎ 202/328-0860, fax 202/328-8730 Woodley Park-Zoo

WINDSOR PARK HOTEL

Rooms in this small hotel are decorated in Queen Anne-style with period art, and each has a small refrigerator. Free Continental breakfast.
E2 ✉ 2116 Kalorama Road NW ☎ 202/483-7700 or 800/247-3064, fax 202/332-4547 Woodley Park-Zoo

WASHINGTON travel facts

Essential Facts *90–91*

Public Transportation *91–92*

Car Rental & Driving *92*

Media & Communications *92–93*

Emergencies *93*

ESSENTIAL FACTS

Airlines

- Major air carriers serving the three airports include:
  Air Canada ☎ 800/776-3000
  Air France ☎ 800/237-2747
  All Nippon Airways ☎ 800/235-9262
  America West ☎ 800/235-9292
  American Airlines ☎ 800/433-7300
  British Airways ☎ 800/247-9297
  Continental ☎ 800/525-0280
  Delta ☎ 800/221-1212
  El Al ☎ 800/223-6700
  Icelandair ☎ 800/223-5500
  Japan Air Lines ☎ 800/525-3663
  KLM Royal Dutch ☎ 800/374-7747
  Lufthansa ☎ 800/645-3880
  Midwest Express ☎ 800/452-2022
  Northwest ☎ 800/225-2525
  Saudi Arabian Airlines ☎ 800/472-8342
  TWA ☎ 800/221-2000
  United ☎ 800/241-6522
  US Airways ☎ 800/428-4322
- For inexpensive flights, contact Southwest Airlines ☎ 800/435-9792.

Customs

- Visitors aged 21 or more may import duty free: 200 cigarettes or 50 cigars or 2kg of tobacco; 1 litre (1 US quart) of alcohol; and gifts up to $100 in value.
- Restricted import items include meat, seeds, plants, and fruit.
- Some medication bought over the counter abroad may be prescription-only in the US and may be confiscated. Bring a doctor's certificate for essential medication.

Electricity

- The electricity supply is 110 volts AC, and plugs are standard two pins. Foreign visitors will need an adaptor and voltage converter for their own appliances.

Etiquette

- Smoking is less and less welcome in Washington. It has been banned from the workplace, and public buildings such as museums and theatres generally do not allow smoking. One exception is Georgetown Mall, where smoking is permitted in the common areas but not in the stores. While most restaurants have separate smoking and nonsmoking sections, some ban it. Bars remain the last bastion of smokers' rights.

Money Matters

- Sales tax in Washington is 5.75 percent on top of the marked goods price.
- Hotel tax ➤ 86.
- Restaurant tax is 10 percent.

Opening Hours

- Shops ➤ 72.
- Banks 🕘 Mon–Fri 9–3, although hours can vary.
- Post offices 🕘 Mon–Fri 8–5; some open Sat for a few hours.

Places of Worship

- Episcopal: Washington National Cathedral ✉ Wisconsin and Massachusetts Avenues NW ☎ 202/537-6200
- Jewish: Adas Israel ✉ Connecticut Avenue and Porter Street NW ☎ 202/362-4433
- Muslim: Islamic Mosque and Cultural Center ✉ 2551 Massachusetts Avenue NW ☎ 202/332-8343
- Roman Catholic: National Shrine of the Immaculate Conception ✉ Michigan Avenue and 4th Street NE ☎ 202/526-8300; Franciscan Monastery ✉ 14th and Quincy Streets NE ☎ 202/526-6800

Public Holidays

- 1 Jan: New Year's Day

- Third Mon in Jan: Birthday of Martin Luther King, Jr
- Third Mon in Feb: Presidents' Day
- Last Mon in May: Memorial Day
- 4 Jul: Independence Day
- First Mon in Sep: Labor Day
- Second Mon in Oct: Columbus Day
- 11 Nov: Veterans Day
- Fourth Thu in Nov: Thanksgiving Day
- 25 Dec: Christmas Day

State Regulations

- You must be 21 years old to drink alcohol in Washington, and you may be required to produce proof of age.

Visitor Information

- Washington, DC, Convention and Visitors Association ✉ 1212 New York Avenue NW, 6th Floor, Washington, DC, 20005 ☎ 202/789-7000, fax 202/789-7037; also ✉ 1300 Pennsylvania Avenue NW ⌚ Enquiries on Sat and Sun
- DC Committee to Promote Washington ✉ 1212 New York Avenue NW, 2nd Floor, Washington, DC, 20005 ☎ 800/422-8644
- National Park Service ✉ Office of Public Affairs, National Capital Region, 1100 Ohio Drive SW, Washington, DC, 20242 ☎ 202/619-7222
- The White House Visitor Center ✉ Baldridge Hall in the Department of Commerce Building, 1450 Pennsylvania Avenue NW ☎ 202/208-1631
- National Park Service information kiosks on the Mall, near the White House, next to the Vietnam Veterans Memorial, and at several other locations throughout the city, can provide helpful information.
- Dial-A-Park is a recording of events at Park Service attractions in and around Washington ☎ 202/619-7275.
- Dial-A-Museum is a recording of exhibits and special offerings at Smithsonian Institution museums ☎ 202/357-2020.

PUBLIC TRANSPORTATION

- The subway (Metro) and bus (Metrobus) systems are run by the Washington Metropolitan Area Transit Authority (WMATA).
- Maps of the Metro system and some bus schedules are available in all Metro stations or at WMATA headquarters ✉ 600 5th Street NW.
- For general information or a copy of *Getting There by Metro*, a helpful brochure, call ☎ 202/637-7000 ⌚ Mon–Fri 6AM–10.30PM; Sat, Sun 8AM–10.30PM.
- Consumer assistance ☎ 202/637-1328 Transit police ☎ 202/962-2121
- For more public transportation and driving information ➤ 6–7.

Buses

- Free bus-to-bus transfers are available from the driver and are good for about 2 hours at designated Metrobus transfer points.

Metro

- Trains run every few minutes ⌚ Mon–Thu 5.30AM–midnight; Fri 5.30AM–1AM; Sat 8AM–1AM; Sun 8AM–midnight.
- The basic fare ($1.10) goes up based on how far you are going and the time of day you are riding (fares are higher during rush hours, 5.30–9.30AM and 3–8PM). Maps in stations tell you both the rush hour fare and regular fare to any destination station.
- Buy a farecard from the machines in the station. The most change

the machine will give you is about $5, so don't use a large note if you are buying a low-value card.

- Insert your farecard into the slot on the side of the turnstile. Retrieve it once the gate opens as you will need it to exit. On exiting, insert the farecard into the turnstile. If your card is for the exact fare the gate will open and you can exit; if your card still has some money on it, it will again pop out the top of the turnstile. A red "STOP" light means you need more money on your card to leave the station and must go the Addfare machine; insert your card and the machine will tell you how much additional fare is owed; pay that fare and return to the exit turnstile.
- The farecards are reusable until the card has a value of less than $1.10. Then, should you need another farecard, your old card can be used as cash in the farecard machine by putting it in the "Used Farecard Trade-In" slot.
- A $5 one-day pass is available for unlimited trips on weekends, holidays or after 9.30AM weekdays. These passes are available at Metro Sales Outlets, including the Metro Center station and some hotels, banks, and grocery stores.
- Transfer to a bus upon leaving the Metro ➤ 6.

Taxis

- If you think that you have been overcharged, ask for the driver's name and cab number and then threaten to call the DC Taxicab Commission ☎ 202/645-6018. If you think you've been over-charged for a ride from the airport, call ☎ 202/331-1671.

Car Rental & Driving

Car Rental

- Alamo ☎ 800/327-9633
  Avis ☎ 800/331-1212; 800/879-2847 in Canada
  Budget ☎ 800/527-0700
  Dollar ☎ 800/800-4000
  Hertz ☎ 800/654-3131
  National ☎ 800/227-7368
- You have to provide a credit card; drivers under 25 years old may have to pay a local surcharge to the hire company.

Driving

- Seat belts ➤ 7.
- Speed limit ➤ 7.
- Although "right turn on red" is permitted, most downtown intersections have signs forbidding it from 7AM–7PM, or banning it outright. Virginia also allows "left turn on red" when turning into a one-way street from another one-way street.
- Parking is a problem in Washington, as the public parking areas fill up quickly with local workers' cars; you might prefer to use public transportation. If you park on city streets, check the signs to make sure it is permitted: Green and white signs show when parking is allowed, red and white signs when it is not. Parking on most main streets is not permitted during rush hours, and if you park illegally your car is likely to get towed. If it does, call ☎ 202/727-5000 to find out where it is and how to get it back.

Media & Communications

Mail

- The National Postal Museum, next door to Union Station, is a working post office ✉ Massachusetts

Avenue and North Capitol Street NE.

- Other branches include: Farragut ✉ 1800 M Street NW ☎ 202/523-2506 Georgetown ✉ 1215 31st Street NW ☎ 202/523-2405 L'Enfant Plaza ✉ 458 L'Enfant Plaza SW ☎ 202/523-2013 Washington Square ✉ 1050 Connecticut Avenue NW ☎ 202/523-2631.

Newspapers & Magazines

- Washington has two major daily newspapers, *The Washington Post* and *The Washington Times*.
- In addition, various neighbourhood weekly newspapers serve Capitol Hill, Georgetown, Adams-Morgan and other areas.
- The *City Paper*, a free weekly with an emphasis on entertainment, is available from newspaper boxes around town and at many restaurants, clubs and other outlets.
- The *Washington Blade*, a free weekly aimed at gays and lesbians, is available at many restaurants, bars and stores, especially in the Dupont Circle, Adams-Morgan, and Capitol Hill areas.
- *Washingtonian*, a monthly magazine, has a calendar of events, dining information, and articles about the city and its prominent people.
- *Where/Washington*, a monthly magazine listing popular things to do, is free at most hotels.
- Other national newspapers are available at newspaper stands.

Telephones

- To call Washington from the UK, dial 00 1, Washington's city code (202), and then the number.
- To call the UK from Washington, dial 011 44, then omit the first zero from the area code.

Emergencies

Embassies & Consulates

- Canada ✉ 501 Pennsylvania Avenue NW ☎ 202/682-1740
- Ireland ✉ 2234 Massachusetts Avenue NW ☎ 202/462-3939
- United Kingdom ✉ 3100 Massachusetts Avenue NW ☎ 202/588-6500, consulate 202/588-7800

Lost Property

- Metro or Metrobus ☎ 202/962-1195
- Smithsonian museums ☎ 202/357-2700
- Other lost articles, check with the police at ☎ 202/727-1010.

Medical Treatment

- The hospital closest to downtown is George Washington University Hospital ✉ 901 23rd Street NW ☎ 202/715-4911, emergencies only.
- 1-800-DOCTORS ☎ 800/362-8677 is a referral service that locates doctors, dentists and urgent-care clinics in the greater Washington area.
- The DC Dental Society operates a referral line ☎ 202/547-7615 🕔 Mon–Fri 8–4.
- CVS operates 24-hour pharmacies ✉ 14th Street and at Thomas Circle NW ☎ 202/628-0720 and ✉ 7 Dupont Circle NW ☎ 202/785-1466.

Safety

- Washington is as safe as any large city. Crime is mainly concentrated far from downtown and the tourist areas.
- At night walk with someone rather than alone; use taxis in less populous areas.

Index

A

accommodations 86–88
Adams-Morgan 24, 71, 72, 81
Adas Israel Congregation 60
African-American sites 52–53
African-American Civil War Memorial and Museum 52
Air and Space Museum, National 43, 54
airports 6–7, 90
Albright, Madeleine K. 13
Alexandria 21
American History, National Museum of 36, 54
Anacostia Museum 52
antiques 76–77
Aquarium, National 54–55
Arboretum, National 59
Archives, National 41
Arlington National Cemetery 26
Art, National Gallery of 42, 59, 83
Arthur M. Sackler Gallery 38
Awakening, The 58

B

baby-sitters 55
bars and lounges 81
Bartholdi Fountain 44
Bet Mish Pachah Synagogue 60
Bethesda 69
Bethune, Mary McLeod 53; Museum and Archives 56
biking 85
Bill of Rights 41
Bishops Garden 58
"Black Broadway" 52
Black History National Recreation Trail 20
boating 85
bookstores 78–79
Botanic Gardens, US 44
Bureau of Engraving and Printing 37
buses 91; tours 20

C

Capital Children's Museum 54
Capitol, US 45
car rental 92
Cedar Hill 50
Chatham Manor 20
Chesapeake and Ohio (C & O) Canal 85
children 54–55
Chinatown 70
cinemas 84
classical music 78–79, 83, 84
climate 4
clothes stores 74
comedy spots 80
concerts 82, 84
Connecticut Avenue 72
Constitution 41
contemporary Washington 10–15
crafts 76–77
Custis-Lee Mansion 26
cybercafés 5

D

dance 84
Declaration of Independence 34, 41
dental treatment 93
disabilities, visitors with 7
Discovery Theater 54
doctors 93
Douglass, Frederick 50; House 52; National Historic Site 50
driving 7, 92–93
Dumbarton Bridge 58
Dumbarton Oaks 58
Dupont Circle 23

E

Eastern Market 72, 75
Einstein Memorial 59
Ellington, "Duke" 52, 53
Emancipation Memorial 53
embassies and consulates 93
emergencies 93
Enfant, Pierre Charles L' 11, 16
entertainment 80–85
events and festivals 4, 83
excursions 20–21

F

Father Patrick Francis Healy Building 52
FBI Building 40
F. D. R. Memorial 34
Folger Shakespeare Library 56
folk entertainment 83
food and drink 64–71, 75, 81
Ford's Theater 82
Fredericksburg 20
Freer Gallery of Art 38
Friendship Arch 58

G

Georgetown 18, 24
Georgetown University 52
golf 85
Grant Memorial 59
guided tours 20

H

Hard Rock Café 54
Hirshhorn Sculpture Garden 59
Historical Society of Washington 56
history 16–17
Holocaust Memorial Museum, US 35, 61
Hotel Washington 62
hotels 62, 67, 86–88
Howard University 52

I

Imani Temple 60
Industrial Bank of Washington 53
insurance 7
Islamic Mosque and Cultural Center 60

J

Jacqueline Kennedy Rose Garden 32
jazz 80
Jefferson Building 48
Jefferson Memorial 34
Jefferson, Thomas 32, 34
Jewish Community Center 60

K

Kennedy Center, John F. 27, 83
Kennedy family graves 26
Key, Francis Scott, bridge 62
King, Jr., Martin Luther 17, 28, 56
Korean War Veterans Memorial 59

L

Library of Congress 48
libraries and archives 56–57
Lincoln, Abraham 28, 45, 48; Memorial 28; Park 53; Theater 52
lost property 93

M

markets 72, 75
Martin Luther King Memorial Library 56
medical treatment 93
Metro 6, 7, 91–92
Metropolitan African Methodist Episcopal Church 60
money 6
Moorland-Spingarn Research Center 56
Morse, Samuel F. B. 16
Mount Vernon 20, 21
Mount Zion Heritage Center and Methodist Church 60
movie theatres 82
murder mystery dinners 80
museum shops 19, 76
music spots 80

N

National Air and Space Museum 43, 54
National Aquarium 54
National Arboretum 59
National Archives 41
National Council of Negro Women 53
National Gallery of Art 42, 61, 83
National Geographic Society 31; Library 56–57
National Mall 13
National Museum of African Art 18
National Museum of American History 36, 54
National Museum of Natural History 54
National Shrine of the Immaculate Conception 49
National Theater 82
National Zoological Park 55
Natural History, National Museum of 54
Navy Museum 55
neighbourhoods 10
newspapers 93
nightlife 24, 80

O

Old Executive Office Building 32
Old Post Office 62
Old Town, Alexandria 20
outdoor spaces 58–59
Olmsted, Frederick Law 14

P

parking 92
parks 58–59
pharmacies 93
Phillips Collection 29
places of worship 60–61, 90
Planet Hollywood 55
political ephemera 19
post offices 92–93
public transportation 5, 91–92
Puppet Company Playhouse 55

R

rail services 91
restaurants 64–71
Rock Creek Park 59

S

Sackler, Arthur M., Gallery 38
St. John's Episcopal Church 61
St. Mary's Episcopal Church 61
St. Matthew's Cathedral 61
sculpture gardens Hirshhorn 59; National Gallery of Art 59
seasons 4
second-hand shopping 77
shopping 18–19, 72–79
Shrine of the Immaculate Conception, National 49
Smithsonian Institution 39, 83; tours 20; libraries 57; museums 29, 31, 35, 36, 38, 39, 41, 42, 43, 48, 50, 52, 54, 55, 56, 57
sightseeing tours 20
smoking 90
sport 85
state regulations 91
Sumner School Museum and Archives 57

T

taxes 90
taxis 92
Temple Micah 61
tennis 85
theatre 82
ticket outlets 82
Tidal Basin 34, 37
time differences 4
Tomb of the Unknowns 26
tours 20–21
trains 91
True Reformers Hall 53

U

U Street 18, 24, 52, 81
Union Station 46
US Botanic Gardens 44
US Capitol 45
US Holocaust Memorial Museum 35, 61
US Supreme Court Building 47
US Treasury 32

V

Vietnam Veterans Memorial 30
views of Washington 62
visitor information 5, 91

W

walks 22–23
walking tours 20
Washington, George Monument 33
Washington Doll's House and Toy Museum 55
Washington Hebrew Congregation 61
Washington National Cathedral 58, 61
Watergate 27
websites 5
White House 32

Z

Zoological Park, National 55

ABOUT THE AUTHORS

Mary Case has lived on Capitol Hill in Washington since being appointed manager of the Smithsonian Institution's 140 million objects and specimens in 1986. In 1992 she began consulting on management issues to the nonprofit arts and cultural community. In 2000 she was appointed academic director of American University's Washington Semester in the Arts. Bruce Walker worked on the weekend section of *The Washington Post* until moving to Los Angles in 2001. He explores the local coastal cities by bicycle and particularly enjoys their diversity of restaurants and nightlife.

Edition Revisers Robin Dougherty, Carole Sugarman (restaurants)
Maps © Automobile Association Developments Limited 2003
Cover Design © Automobile Association Developments Limited 2003

A CIP catalogue record for this book is available from the British Library.

ISBN 0 7495 3572 5

Published by AA Publishing, a trading name of Automobile Association Developments Limited, whose registered office is Millstream, Maidenhead Road, Windsor, Berkshire, SL4 5GD. Registered number 1878835.

First published 1996. Second edition 1998. Third edition 2000. Fourth edition 2003.

Colour separation by Daylight Colour Art Pte Ltd., Singapore
Printed and bound by Dai Nippon Printing Co. (Hong Kong) Ltd.

ACKNOWLEDGEMENTS
The Automobile Association would like to thank the following photographers, libraries and associations for their assistance in the preparation of this book:
BRIDGEMAN ART LIBRARY Peacock Room by James McNeill Whistler, 1876–7, Freer Gallery, Smithsonian Institute Washington USA 38t; M. GOSTELOW 59; HULTON ARCHIVE 17l, 17r; MARY EVANS PICTURE LIBRARY 16/17, 38b; MRI BANKERS GUIDE TO FOREIGN CURRENCY 6; PETER NEWARK'S AMERICAN PICTURES 16l, 16c; THE PHILLIPS COLLECTION 29; SPECTRUM COLOUR LIBRARY 43b; STOCKBYTE 5; WASHINGTON, DC CONVENTION AND TOURISM CORPORATION 1b, 10c, 24c, 24r. The remaining pictures are held in the Association's own library (AA PHOTO LIBRARY) and were taken by ETHEL DAVIS with the exception of back cover, US Capitol Building, 1t, 2, 4, 6, 7l, 7c, 8bl, 8/9, 9t, 9c, 9b, 10t, 11t, 11c, 12t, 12c, 12/13, 13r, 14t, 14c, 15l, 15r, 16t, 18t, 19t, 19c, 20tl, 22tl, 24t, 24l, 34b, which were taken by CLIVE SAWYER.

A01084
Fold out map © Mairs Geographischer Verlag / Falk Verlag, 73751 Ostfildern
Transport map © TCS, Aldershot, England

TITLES IN THE CITYPACK SERIES
• Amsterdam • Bangkok • Barcelona • Beijing • Berlin • Boston • Brussels & Bruges •
• Chicago • Dublin • Florence • Hong Kong • Lisbon • Ljubljana • London • Los Angeles •
• Madrid • Melbourne • Miami • Montréal • Munich • New York • Paris • Prague • Rome •
• San Francisco • Seattle • Shanghai • Singapore • Sydney • Tokyo • Toronto • Venice •
• Vienna • Washington DC •